S. SEKOU A

C000284827

D R E A M S
DECODED
REVELATION, INTERPRETATION
AND APPLICATION

DREAMS DECODED

Revelation, Intepretation and Application

Sekou Publishing
sekou@sekou.me

Copyright © 2016 by Sekou Abodunrin

Cover Design and Page Layout
Kenteba Kreations
www.kentebakreations.com

ISBN: 978-0-9575677-7-1

Published by Sekou Publishing. All rights reserved.

Unless otherwise indicated, all Scripture quotations are taken from the King James Version of the Bible.

Scripture quotations marked (MIRROR) are taken from MIRROR BIBLE. Copyright © 2012

Scripture quotations marked (AMPLIFIED) are taken from the Amplified® Bible, Copyright © 1954, 1958, 1962, 1964, 1965, 1987 by The Lockman Foundation. Used by permission. www.lockman.org

Scripture quotations marked (GOODSPEED) are taken from The New Testament: An American Translation by Edgar J. Godspeed (Copyright © 1923, 1948 by the University of Chicago)

The author has emphasized some words in Scripture quotations in bold type.

Christ is the language of God's logic. Let his message sink into you with unlimited vocabulary, taking wisdom to its most complete conclusion. This makes your fellowship an environment of instruction in an atmosphere of music. Every lesson is a reminder, echoing in every song you sing, whether it be a psalm or a hymn or a song in the spirit. Grace fuels your heart with inspired music to the Lord.
Colossians 3:16 (MIRROR)

Contents

Introduction

D reams, everyone has these internal movies that play for us when we close our eyes in sleep. Most of us will have tens of thousands of dreams throughout our lifetime. We are told that on the average, we spend about 6 years of our lives dreaming. This represents over 2,000 days spent in that other world.

Dream scientists tell us that every human dreams – whether adults or foetuses in the womb dreams at least one hour daily when sleeping at night. They have shown that we sleep in 90-minute cycles.

This book does not study sleep science. It does not explore the scientific aspects of sleep. It does not also approach man from a purely clinical, chemical or biological perspective. It presents a view from a spiritual standpoint.

The word "dream" comes from an old English word that means music and joy. Studies have shown that our brain waves are more active when we are in the dream state than when we are otherwise awake. Some experts have also suggested that toddlers do not dream about themselves and that they do not appear in their own dreams.

Dreams remain one of those controversial subjects in the church world at large, even today. Though much has been written about dreams in both the secular and religious press, much of what the scriptures reveal about dreams have been ignored!

On one end of the spectrum, there are those who believe that all dreams are the product of yesterday's left-over pizza and at the other extreme there are those who believe that every minute detail of every dream is bursting with divine revelation. One camp would have us treat all dreams as garbage while the other group would have us pay attention to every dream and treat them as guidance from God. Do we join one of these camps? As with many things in life, the truth is somewhere in-between those two extremes.

This book might disappoint those who desire to have their whole lives governed by dreams. It might also not be easy reading for those who propose that God has done away with dreams altogether.

This book aims to contribute to a sane, scriptural understanding of dreams. It is true that there are a lot of troublesome practices peddled around today concerning dreams and their interpretation. We must not let this stop us from a scriptural examination of dreams. We must be careful not to throw away the baby with the bath water.

This is written in order that we might recover our dreams from the grip of mysticism and myths and ground it in the truth of God's Word. The bible is still the standard by which we must measure our dreams.

We write this trusting that God would use it to clear up confusion and bring needed clarity on this subject for His own glory.

Kent, England. 2016.

Appreciation

To all those whose hearts are awake while their eyes close in sleep.

The Greater One Within

The real requirement of God is not rules and regulations contained within stone tablets. Even after the fall, Adam could hear God and talk to God and so could Cain after murdering Abel. Every Christian already hears God's voice. The challenge is not whether God will lead us.

We do not grow up spiritually in order that God might lead us. We grow in our ability to recognize and follow His voice. When we say that God is leading us, we do not mean that is when God speaks. We mean we are recognizing that which He has already communicated. We don't make God lead us, we improve in our recognition of what He has conveyed.

Jesus said, "the sheep hear his voice: and he calleth his own sheep by name" (John 10:3b). By this He means that we live by

His voice and not by rules and laws. We only turn to rules and regulations when we stop hearing His voice.

His voice operates from within our spiritual nature in the born again spirit today.

His voice is real to us because we are the offspring of God.

My darling children, you have nothing to fear; do not doubt for a moment the legitimacy of your sonship! You originate in God and have already conquered the worldly religious system because of the unveiling of Christ in you! His living presence in you is far superior to the futile anti-Christ mindsets present in the world.
1 John 4:4 (MIRROR)

Notice that John does not speak of God in the heavens above or the hills and mountains. God, who made this vast universe, has made His home in the Christian. God has already made the Christian a master. The reality of God's indwelling is a greater spiritual fact than His creation of the physical universe. It is baffling that we have more songs of His creating the sun, moon and stars than we have of His mighty indwelling. Unconsciously, this is because we lightly esteem the Word of God. We sing of that of which we are very sure. We are to acknowledge how big God is in us.

The epistles are not big on God being the creator of the heavens. The epistles insist that God is the creator of the new creation. We are God's handiwork.

God wants us to know that He is in us. He is trying to get us to become conscious of Himself. God is in our words, in our touch and in our actions. We can communicate God. We are not afraid of any devil in our wakeful moments or when we are asleep for that matter. The facts of Redemption are the same whether we are awake or asleep.

The Lord Jesus expected the Holy Spirit to do more after His resurrection than He had done during His earth walk. Since we are joint heirs with Christ, we expect the Spirit to be more powerful in us because of the resurrection of Jesus than when He was in the earthly ministry of Jesus. God is as available to us as He is to the Lord Jesus who is the head of the Church.

God did not give us His power with the intent that we idle around, waiting for His direction before we use that power. God's intent is that we use His power for His glory because we are sons of the Father. This is what it means for God to be in you. It is the triumphant dominating Spirit of God in man.

On the basis of this overcoming ability, we have a spiritual responsibility to command rest upon our bodies in the name of Jesus, close our eyes and then receive sweet sleep (See Prov. 3:24).

The spirit of the born again one is godlike and kingly. This is because in the New Birth, the spirit of the born again one bears God's image. The spirit is the real man and is not asleep in much the same way that God never slumbers nor sleeps (Psalm 121:4). This means that while your body is asleep, your spirit is very much awake.

This is a spiritual fact.

God wants us to brag on the reality of His indwelling. The Christian is God's postcode. In England, you can locate any house by knowing its postcode. If a man were to give you his postcode, you would definitely know where to locate him. You are God's address. You are His location on the earth and you represent Him in your world. You are the embodiment of God

The greater one is in me just as He was with the Lord Jesus. The indwelling of God means that since I am subject to God, every demon, devil or evil spirit is subject to me. They are subject to me in the same manner that they are subject to the Lord Jesus.

You do not permit any naughty demon strike fear into your heart because the Lord has not given you a spirit of fear. There is no fear in your spiritual DNA.

We are fully indwelt by God, therefore, we do not have half the Holy Ghost. This is why we know that we are masters. God Himself is the guarantee of our mastery. He is our sponsor. He has translated us from the dominion of darkness and lifted us up to the highest at the right hand of majesty.

On the basis of these spiritual facts, we have assurance from God's Word that our hands are not tied just because we dream while our eyes are closed in sleep.

You are to become God-inside minded.

Taste Not, Touch Not

Not understanding the implication of God's indwelling, some people are afraid of everything. They are even afraid of eating in their sleep though they eat while awake. They allow myths and mysticism rob them of the riches of God's Word.

Who satisfieth thy mouth with good things; so that thy youth is renewed like the eagle's.
Psalm 103:5

God puts His Word in our mouths and uses this to energize us. The truth contained within this Psalm is not suspended just because you go to bed. God continues to put His Word in my mouth even in my dreams.

We see that the Apostle John ate in his great vision (See Rev 10:10). That spiritual food, which he ate in a vision, was the impartation of divine power to prophesy. Ezekiel also ate in his vision until his belly was full (see Ezek. 3:3). You'll find that all the people that ate in their visions in the bible were saints. None of them thought demons were feeding them. A saint does not reason that way.

I don't eat much in daily life but if I were to eat in my sleep, just like Ezekiel and John, I'll make sure I eat a lot. It is the table of God's provision.

Someone says, "What if it is the demons giving you food?"

Well, what does the Word say?

The Word says that God prepares a table before me in the presence of mine enemies (Ps. 23:5)! The bible does not say that God withdraws His table of provision when we sleep.

The redemption that we have in Christ is the grounds of our confidence. God never withdraws this confidence for He is the ground and the foundation of it. We can however, cast away this confidence (Heb. 10:35). It is those traditions and myths that we embrace that cause us to cast away our confidence.

When Paul instructed that evil communication corrupts, he was saying that the communication of evil (wrong doctrine) corrupts and weakens our conscience. This seduces us away from the boldness that comes from knowing what Christ has done. (See

1 Cor. 15:33).

If you believe that demons feed you in your dream it is because of the teachings you have been exposed to. That kind of doctrine weakens your conscience. . This is evil communication. There are things that God does not forbid but limited knowledge in the soul creates and enforces myths that forbid it. Eating in and of itself, whether asleep or awake, should not be a big deal (gluttony is). Our conscience can make a big deal of it. If you are going to make a big deal of it, side in with God's Word. Receive your food with thanksgiving and prayer (see 1 Tim. 4:4). You should be a person of prayer, even in your sleep. Solomon prayed to God in his dream.

Dear friends, if our consciences do not condemn us, we approach God with confidence
1 John 3:21 (GOODSPEED)

Without a doubt, conscience and knowledge go hand in hand. It is your conscience that withdraws or supplies boldness and confidence. If your conscience condemns you on a matter, it withdraws confidence and you feel guilt (see 1 John 3:21). If your conscience is weak in an area, you won't be bold in that area. Your conscience is not necessarily God leading you.

We receive condemnation from our heart and think that is God talking to us through that sense of condemnation. You only feel condemned for eating in your dream because you have been instructed that it is an evil thing. Though you cannot find scripture for such beliefs you still let it govern your emotional state.

We don't go about ignoring our conscience. We diligently subject our conscience to God's Word so that the Word cleanses our conscience and strips it of myths and old wives fables. We use

God's Word to redesign our conscience to align with God's Word and the dominion we have in Christ.

The kind of teaching that stirs up fear in people for eating in their dream is actually one of the prophesied signs of the end times. It is a doctrine of devils to command people not to eat meats asleep or awake. People that adhere to such have departed from the faith. People attach a lot of spiritual weight to these old wives fables. This ends up searing their conscience (see 1 Tim. 4).

People with a weak conscience are those that act on other people's convictions rather than getting into the Word of God and using God's Word to build theirs (see 1 Cor. 8).

If I were to find myself eating in my dream, I'll eat conscious that greater is He who is in me than he who is in the world! I'll agree with the Word that nothing is to be refused (asleep or awake), if it were received with thanksgiving (see 1 Tim. 4:4). Nothing can penetrate the immunity that is mine in the finished work of Christ. This is enforced by faith in the security that is mine in Christ. The anointing that accompanies the New Birth dematerializes any yoke. Enough said about old wives fables.

This book discusses dreams from a scriptural standpoint. By dreams, I am referring to the series of thoughts, transactions and activities that we perceive to be real in our inner life while we are fast asleep.

Many superstitious Christians awake out of their dreams and immediately make decisions or alter their lives based upon the dream they just had. In the same way that it would be silly to read something on the internet and then alter your life based on what you have read, it is silly to take decisions based on dreams without first analyzing them in the light of God's Word. It is the content of our dreams and visions that are important. No matter how sophisticated a dream sounds, it must always be judged by God's Word.

So then faith cometh by hearing, and hearing by the word of God.
Rom 10:17

It is clear then that faith's source is found in the content of the message heard; the message is Christ.
Rom 10:17 (MIRROR)

The Word of God is a container for faith. It is an information source just like myths, traditions and the circumstances of life are information sources. The more you hear the Word, the more bible faith you have at your disposal for everyday living.

The more you hear about the ministry of Christ, the more you'll believe that ministry. You are to have more faith in the ministry of Christ to you than you have in satan's ministry of condemnation against you. The more you hear yourself boldly declare the supremacy of Christ's ministry to you, the harder it becomes for satan to penetrate through the hedge of protection that surrounds you in Christ.

What we believe is based on what we have heard and continue to hear. Our beliefs then form our experiences. Thus we experience things in line with what we believe as a result of the teachings that we are exposed to.

This is why people do not receive eternal life and get born again where the gospel has not been preached (Rom. 10:14). It is also why people do not speak in tongues in churches that do not teach about it. Whether men get born again or speak in tongues is not up to God. It is up to us to give men the gospel. When they hear and believe the gospel it empties divine power into their lives. Our lives mirror what we continue to hear and believe.

This principle is why people tend to have an unhealthy dream life until through the gospel, they discover that their dream lives do not have to be ruled by myths, tradition and fear. It is a spiritual fact that the heart of a man will conform his dream life to reproduce more of what he hears whether he is a saint or sinner..

The power to stabilize our dreams is contained within the gospel as we expose ourselves to it and believe it.

I meet too many Christians who think that they have a dream problem or a sleep problem even. The real issue is that these Christians have areas where they have not heard or believed the truth of God's Word. They have fed on myths and traditions until they became afraid of the devil and what he can do to them in the arena of sleep.

Just like faith, unbelief comes by what we hear. Our religious traditions dress satan with borrowed clothes of omnipotence that is foreign to satan himself. When we acknowledge the devil's power, he becomes as big to us as we believe him to be. We are to acknowledge the greater one within! Whether asleep or awake our spirits are still masters.

Beloved, believe not every spirit, but try the spirits whether they are of
God: because many false prophets are gone out into the world.
1 John 4:1

The faith you exercise in a spirit being is a product of what you hear about that spirit. Feast heavily on the Word of God. You cannot be afraid of the devil if your information about him is from God's Word.

As a general principle, spirit beings draw their energy from the faith that you exercise in them. What you believe about a spirit being commissions that being in your life. If you do not like what you are co-creating in your life, change what you have been hearing and believing.

Do not be afraid of any force, influence or energy when you go to bed.

When you are confident that you have every resource to win in life whether asleep or awake, it is safe to go to sleep. This is because you are confident of God's ability invested in you and of the godlike dominion radiating out of the consciousness of the greater one indwelling you.

Realities flowing from the spirit to the soul

And the very God of peace sanctify you wholly; and I pray God your whole spirit and soul and body be preserved blameless unto the coming of our Lord Jesus Christ.
1 Thessalonians 5:23

Greek scholars tell us that the phrase, "I pray" is not in the Greek. Therefore Paul was not praying at all in this verse. He was not praying that God would do that which is His job to do - and neither should we! Paul was stating a fact of redemption - God's faithfulness to preserve man in the dimensions of man's being.

Man is a phenomenal creation of God who is able to operate on three dimensions simultaneously.

In the visible components of our nature, we have a body just like animals have a body. We function in the physical, psychical and spirit dimensions through our body, soul and spirit respectively.

Man is a spirit just like God and angels are spirits. Man is a spiritual being. The fundamental part of man, which is also to be his dominant part, is his spirit. As a Christian, he is a son of God.

There is a divine reality of dominion within our spirits that has not made it into our souls. Christians that reason carnally are only willing to go by the evidence of their senses. If they feel it, then it is real; otherwise, it is fiction. They have a low estimation of divine things, for divine things are contacted through the Word of God.

In the New Birth, the human spirit has God's DNA. God is not creating human spirits in heaven and looking for which wombs to send them into on the earth. God gave that power to Adam and his offspring. It is in the New Birth that God gets involved in creating a human spirit.

Notice that the correct order is spirit, soul and then body. God works from the invisible. We work in the visible. What God has done in the invisible is complete and perfect. As we hear about what He has accomplished, it changes our minds and releases that complete dominion from our spirits into our souls and bodies.

Consider some spiritual realities about man;

Blessed is the man to whom the Lord will not impute sin.
Romans 4:8
How blessed is the man who receives a receipt instead of an invoice for his
sins.
Romans4:8 (MIRROR)

The gospel message is that God has already reconciled us to Himself and we cannot increase in favor with Him. The gospel is scandalous to the unrenewed mind.

There is an important principle involved here.

Jesus will not be sacrificed afresh for our sins. He was sacrificed once and for all (Heb. 10:10). This is why God will not impute sin to us. God has forgiven us of all our sins for all time. God has seen to it that sins as well as the sin nature have no place in our recreated spirits. God is not about to forgive; He has completely forgiven us in Christ (Eph. 4:32). This is the blessing of righteousness. Our righteousness is not performance based. We are created righteous in Christ in the New Birth.

God responds to our errors with His mercy and is not holding our sins against us (2 Cor. 5:19).

The adverse consequences we experience for our sins are not because God is keeping any record of them. It is not down to God. God has said that He will not impute sin against us. We take Him at His Word. He has said He will not; therefore, we know He never will.

Know ye not, that to whom ye yield yourselves servants to obey, his servants ye are to whom ye obey; whether of sin unto death, or of obedience unto righteousness?
Romans 6:16

Our sins affect us in the soul realm.

Satan holds our sins against us. This he uses as his access into our souls and bodies. We do not live holy because we are trying to dodge God's wrath. One of the reasons we live holy is because we are aware of the havoc sin has on our soulish and bodily constitution. We want to limit satan's access to our soul realm in particular. When we change our minds to agree with God's Word, we increase the footprint of the manifest presence of God in our lives. We crowd out satan. Repentance removes satan's advantage from our soul. It slows down his advance and pulls out the rug from under his feet so to speak.

Likewise, I say unto you, there is joy in the presence of the angels of God
over one sinner that repenteth.
Luke 15:10

Repentance on earth inspires joy and rejoicing in Heaven. I would expect a saint who has been redeemed and therefore knows the power of repentance to be more stirred than an angel. The concept of redemption and repentance are foreign to angels. Those "angels" rejoicing in heaven must be saints who have passed on before. This rejoicing "in the presence of the angels" would be a reference to the joy that the saints in heaven experience as the news flows through that someone on earth has agreed with God's way of thinking.

When a Christian yields to sinful lusts, he is really yielding to a "whom". That whom is not God but satan. Once we yield to satan, he gladly imputes this against us. This gives him the access to wreak havoc. He is not that powerful, we are that yielded! This is what releases the wrong spiritual forces in our lives. This principle still works though God is actually not imputing any sin to us. God is not permitting anything, we are. God is not the one permitting you to have a scary dream life nor is He using it to teach you. Tradition insists that God is in control of your dreams when He is not. Using this principle of empowering what we yield to, God wants us to use our will to yield to Him in order that His power might be unleashed in our souls and bodies.

If you have been yielding to satan, you repent of that by agreeing with God's Word. As you yield your will to the gospel, which is the power of God (Rom. 1:16), you place a demand on God's power to flow out of your recreated spirit into your life and bring peace.

Though it appears to the casual observer that things happen randomly in our world, the truth is that our permission is needed in order for certain expressions to persist in our world.

Demons by themselves cannot influence the natural dimension except through human beings. They do this through the soul of man. It is as we yield our will that we permit spirits to manifest in our world. What you allow to stay in the doorway of your soul will attract equivalent spirits.

It is true that the spirit realm influences our physical world.

This is not because these spirits have tremendous power. It is because we yield to them. We yield with our will. Whatever you yield to, you give authority to express in your world. Authority flows in the opposite direction to yielding.

Only a spirit with a physical body can bring change upon the earth. It is as we yield to God that we widen His footprint in our lives.

Fear cannot co-exist in this love realm. The perfect love union that we are talking about expels fear. Fear holds on to an expectation of crisis and judgment and interpret it as due punishment [a form of karma!] It echoes torment and only registers in someone who does not realise the completeness of their love union.
1 John 4:18 (MIRROR)

Love and fear are opposites. Hell is the perfection of fear. Fear has torment. It is the fear in our soul that attracts the wrong type of spirits who inject the wrong thoughts and desires into our thought stream. Dwelling on these wrong thoughts empower them to become strong desires (James. 1:14). The evil spirits feed off the strength of these desires to inspire us to act wrong. Our actions then give these spirits expression in the physical realm. These spirits derive their energy from our fear. It is as we yield our will to the power of God's love in us that our minds become less penetrable by these thoughts, which try to distort God's original thought flowing through our inner life.

Fear sets our wills against our spirits and hinders us from experiencing the peace, victory and dominion that is already within our spirits. The love of God helps our wills stay yielded to our spirits. This aids the constant flow of supply from our invisible realm into the visible parts of our being.

The Rich Man & Lazarus

L uke records an interesting story spoken by the Lord Jesus about the experiences of two Jews beyond the grave. I often use this to illustrate the reality of the spiritual components of man.

There is much debate about whether to treat this as a parable or as a description of real events. Sometimes it is easy to tell that what we reading in the bible is a parable or a real event. At other times, it is not so easy to tell the difference.

Jesus once said, "Destroy this temple, and in three days I will raise it up" (John 2:19).

The Jews who heard this were confused because they took this statement literally when Jesus meant it as figurative speech. He was not referring to the magnificent temple in which the congregation of Israel held their meetings. That physical temple took forty-six years to build!

Jesus was speaking of the temple of His body (John 2:21).

He expected His hearers to understand this subtle fact.

We are able to identify this statement about pulling down the temple as parabolic speech because we have explanations included in the text of the bible for our benefit.

However, it is not always immediately obvious from the text that we are reading a parable.

The passage of the Rich Man and Lazarus comes after four other parables (of the lost sheep, lost coin, prodigal son and unjust steward). Interestingly, Luke refers to all these as a single parable. He does not say that Jesus spoke parables unto the people. He said, "And he spake this parable unto them," (Luke 15:3). Jesus was emphasising one grand thought throughout but presented it from different perspectives. This means that each of these stories are really portions of a single parable.

Unlike His other parables, this would be the only one that uses facts from the afterlife. It also mentions people by name – Abraham and Lazarus.

I must quickly point out in passing that in this parable, if we can call it a parable, Jesus doesn't primarily set out to teach about man's multi-dimensional nature. The Lord Jesus is specifically rebuking the Pharisees and Jews, who could not see that God wanted to show mercy to all – Jew and non-Jew alike.

There was a certain rich man,

Which was clothed in purple and fine linen   Luke 16:19

He was one of Abraham's seed   Luke 16:24

Had five brothers who lived in their father's house
[Luke 16:27,28]

And had Moses and the prophets [Luke 16:25]

But did not listen to Moses or the prophets [Luke 16:29]

Would not be convinced if someone rose from the dead
[Luke 16:31]

The parable of the unjust steward, which came before this, teaches us that we are to be good stewards of God's resources. It also teaches that we are to use our stewardship to further God's kingdom. We plan for our eternal future by making use of the mammon of unrighteousness to make friends. These friends are those lives that we invested into with the resources at our disposal (see Luke 16:1-12).

The rich man made provision for his time on earth only. He did not use the resources that he had at his disposal to make Lazarus a friend who would welcome him in the eternal habitations. Thus, the rich man lived only for himself. We know that the Rich knew Lazarus for he mentions Lazarus by name when discussing with Abraham.

Nothing is said directly about the spiritual condition of either the Rich Man or Lazarus though much can be inferred.

It would be wrong to say that Lazarus obtained comfort in Abraham's bosom through his poverty on earth or that the Rich Man was damned because of his wealth. This is not what the story or the bible itself teaches.

The Rich Man

We notice that the rich man has five brothers. Since we know that Abraham calls the Rich Man a son, we only have to find out which of Abraham's sons had five brothers. The bible declares that Jacob's wife Leah had six sons of which Judah was one. Therefore, Judah had five brethren (see Genesis 35:22-26).

On the other hand, the brothers of this Rich Man could be in reference to the Sadducees and Pharisees or to the five brothers of the High Priest. It is also possible that the reference to five brothers does not mean anything.

God wanted the whole nation to be a kingdom of priests unto God (Ex. 19:6). The rich man could be a general reference to the kingdom of Judah who both supplied the king (purple) as well as the priesthood (linen). The Rich Man feeding sumptuously every day means that as a nation, they were daily supplied with the rich mercies of Jehovah who gave them the sacred scriptures and promises (see Romans 9:3-5).

We observe that David had prophesied that the table of provision from which this Rich Man fed sumptuously was going to become a trap for them later. Thus, David knew by the Spirit that a reversal was coming (see Romans 11:9).

Bible students know that linen is the cloth of the highly privileged priesthood of Israel (see Lev. 16:4). More specifically, this Rich Man could be a reference to the Jewish High Priest because the High Priest was the only man in Israel that dressed in purple and fine linen.

While the Rich Man could see Lazarus in Abraham's bosom, we are not told that Lazarus could see the Rich Man.

Lazarus

Moreover the dogs came and licked his sores. Luke 16:21b

Scholars tell us that the Greek word translated moreover here is better translated as others.

Thus that verse should read, "Other dogs came and licked his sores". Which would mean that Lazarus was also a dog!

In covenant terms, Lazarus was as much a dog as the dogs that licked his sores. Lazarus therefore, did not start out as a seed of Abraham. Lazarus saw himself as a beggar, while the Rich Man saw him as a dog. The point is that though God wanted all the nations of the earth blessed, Israel was working against this happening. Israel was to be a light to the nations (See Isaiah 49:6).

Lazarus is at the gate and not at the table with the Rich Man, thus he is far removed from the Rich Man. Since he is placed at the gate, we conclude that Lazarus is too weak to carry himself or worse still he is crippled.

Since he eats with the other dogs and sits at the gate of the Rich man, Lazarus represents that which is not part of the commonwealth of Israel. He is representative of that which is outside the gate of the seed of Abraham. Lazarus is not clothed in purple but in sores (Luke 16:20). This means he did not have the same privileges as the Rich man. His standing and status was different. The point is that they were worlds apart. This is emphasized by the fact that there is a great gulf fixed between the Rich man and Lazarus after death.

Interestingly, Lazarus is the Greek form of the name Eleazar. In the Old Testament, Eleazar was the servant who could not be Abraham's heir (Gen. 15:2). Eleazar (or Lazarus) is the one for whom there is no inheritance.

The Message

Though he is a genetic son of Abraham, the Rich Man sees Abraham afar off. He is a seed of Abraham, who ends up being far from Abraham. Thus, this Jew does not end up where he started. On the other hand, Lazarus does not start out with the privileges that the rich man and his brothers started out with in their father's house (See Rom. 9:4).

The rich man is persuaded that someone had to rise from the dead in order for the people to believe. This is because the Jew seeks a sign (1 Cor. 1:22). Jesus gave them the sign of the prophet Jonah (Mt. 12:39). We know from the book of Acts that when Israel heard the message of the resurrection that the Pharisees, Sadducees and their hearers did not believe.

Scholars tell us that the word Lazarus means the Lord will help me. The point is that the Lord is helping Lazarus though he is not clothed in linen. Lazarus has no priesthood, yet the Lord helps him in mercy.

The fact that the Rich Man died and was buried means that

His former privileges are forever buried. This is Jesus' way of saying that the Rich Man experiences a change of condition. A whole way of dealing is over forever. Jesus is using the story to represent the death of both the Rich Man and Lazarus to the conditions that had given privilege to the Rich Man in the first place. The death of Christ changes everything. It is death with Christ that confers eternal benefits.

Thus, there are enough hints in this parable that teaches the coming reversal of roles between those who are Abraham's seed according to the flesh and those who were not. In other words, the first would be last and the last first. Abraham pointed the Rich Man to scriptures. The real issue was whether men believed the scriptures or not. The Rich Man believed in outward evidences. He thought his wealth was proof of spirituality. Poverty does not send a man to heaven any more than wealth sends a man to hell.

Spiritual privilege would no longer be based on membership in Israel but death with Christ.

It is noteworthy that in response to the rich man's thirst for a sign, Abraham tells the rich man, "They have Moses and the prophets" (see Luke 16:29). Abraham was referring to the Old Testament scriptures. Abraham understood that the Word of God gives a stronger foundation and represented higher spiritual authority than any other spiritual experience.

The Rich Man thought that signs and wonders could do more than the Word of God! In other words, people abide in unbelief because their heart is hardened by unbelief. Peter preached about the resurrection of Jesus. He grounded it on scriptures. The people were to believe the Word.

Observe closely that the parable does not focus on Lazarus'

fellowship with Abraham but with the drastic reversal of the Rich Man's fortunes. The Rich Man made two requests, both of which required Lazarus to do something - both were denied.

Life beyond the veil

Nevertheless, as God's Word is multi-layered revelation, this story is loaded with meaning for the discerning listener.

Since the Lord Jesus does not end the story of the Rich Man at his burial, we can also glean some facts about life beyond the veil as well as some insight into the spiritual components of man's anatomy. There is more to man than cells, bone tissue and muscle.

The store of memory

But Abraham said, Son, remember that thou in thy lifetime receivedst thy good things, and likewise Lazarus evil things: but now he is comforted, and thou art tormented.
Luke 16:25

The ability to remember shows that thoughts do not stop existing after death. Since the brain is buried in the grave, the implication is that thoughts exist outside the brain. Your thoughts will outlive your physical body. Memory is a function of the soul. Thus, we can tell that the spirit retains the soul at death. The soul goes wherever the spirit goes. The soul is so tied to the spirit before and after death that only God's Word has the power to separate soul and spirit (see Heb. 4:12). Even when we leave our bodies in death, our spirit and soul will go together.

Abraham expected the man to be able to recall events from his time on earth. Since the brain was dissolved in the dust of the earth, it must mean that there is a non-biological component in man aside from the brain that stores memories which can then be remembered beyond the grave. The fact that Abraham expected the rich man to "remember" implies that thoughts existed in the unseen realm, so that even when the natural storage in their brain is dead, these thoughts live on and can be interacted with. The grave does not wipe our memories.

This story hints at the fact that there is more to numeracy than the brain. We know this to be the case since the rich man could count the number of brothers that he had on earth though he was no longer in possession of his brain. His brain had been buried prior to this conversation. We also notice the fact that though this man no longer had a brain, he could still correctly access his earthly experiences at will.

Since the Rich Man knew Lazarus and recalled that he had five brothers in his father's house, we know that there is continuity of memory that we carry over from our time on the earth. This shows that memory is a basic element of personality. This establishes that beyond the grave, we are not different people but the same people marvelously relocated and transformed. Heaven does not erase our person.

Though the brain and the soul are linked, the soul is able to recall facts without the brain. The brain is unable to express intelligence without the soul.

This would mean that our memories are stored within our soul and not merely within our brains.

Memory is stored in the invisible components of man. This is a permanent type of storage. Memory is accessible beyond the grave. We are accustomed in the present life to accessing that storage though the brain. In a sense, if we borrow from the world of computing, you could liken the soul of man to a computer's hard disk. In that sense, the brain would be the RAM.

Burial does not imply the death of memory or that everything is over. A significant chapter is definitely closed. Another door opens beyond the grave.

While declared to be brain dead, clinically dead and dead in every way known to man, there are several reports of people who have recounted being able to recall minute details of their lives flashing in front of them like a compressed movie. Many are even able to recount the events going on in the hospital ward while they were brain dead!

We observe that our memories are stored in our soul and are accessed through our brains.

Since the Rich Man saw Abraham afar off it is possible to experience spiritual distance and perspective. Distance does not mean the same thing to spiritual beings as it does to beings with a physical body. Spiritual distance is not the same thing as physical distance.

Furthermore, a spirit being is unaware of clock time as we experience it in a physical body. Our bodies understand clock time while our spirits do not. Spiritual time flows forwards and backwards while clock time flows only forwards. I believe that God created this earth with clock time while He created spirits in spiritual time.

In a psychological sense, Joy makes time brief while sorrow

makes time seem long. Thus our spiritual state is how we experience time in the spirit realm. All time whether spiritual or physical flows from God as its ultimate source.

Transfer of information

Abraham saith unto him, They have Moses and the prophets; let them hear them. And he said, Nay, father Abraham: but if one went unto them from the dead, they will repent. And he said unto him, If they hear not Moses and the prophets, neither will they be persuaded, though one rose from the dead.
Luke 16:29-31

While conversations between Abraham and the rich man are documented, we can only assume that Lazarus and Abraham must have talked, though we are not told about the manner of conversation that they had. Since the body of the Rich Man had been buried and yet Abraham was having conversations with the Rich Man, we conclude that it is not the body that confers on man the power to have conversations.

The ordinary reading of the statements of Jesus concerning the conversation between Abraham and the Rich Man is that conversation was normal. The spirits and souls of men are capable of conversations.

Since Abraham knew spiritual facts that the rich man was unaware of, it shows that there are varying degrees of comprehension beyond the grave. We will all know more beyond the grave but some people will know beyond others, as we will all develop spiritually at different rates.

This conversation was across a considerable distance for the rich man saw Abraham afar off (Luke 16:23). Yet in spite of this, both the rich man and Abraham conversed, both instantly understanding each other. If we allow for the fact that Abraham and the rich man were not the only ones having conversations at that point in time, it becomes all the more intriguing how to pin point the exact nature of the mode of communication between Abraham and the Rich Man. Was everyone else listening in on this discourse? If not, how could these two maintain a verbal conversation across the great divide with all the noise around them?

Their communion could not have been verbal. If it was, there would be a lot of pandemonium and noise. This is primarily a conversation between spirits. Spiritual communion is on a higher level beyond the limitations of earthly language. It is almost as though they communicated beyond spoken language, in much the same way a man would look across the room at a woman he is in love with and without words he could "speak" volumes to her. It would appear that Abraham and the rich man understood each other via spiritual impressions and thoughts. Thoughts and impressions are more accurate forms of spiritual communion and they are instantly recognized and interpreted in the spirit realm. Spiritual communion carries images, perceptions and meaning simultaneously.

We notice that Abraham had been dead for about 250 years by the time Moses was born and that the rich man lived long after Moses' death. The rich man and Abraham were not contemporaries. Notwithstanding, the rich man seemed to instantly recognize Abraham, for he called him "Father Abraham". Such recognition cannot be a function of memory but a characteristic of the human spirit.

It is obvious that Abraham knew about Moses and the prophets though their ministry was non-existent while he was on earth.

He must have obtained this knowledge after his death. Thus the development of the soul of man and its grasp of spiritual facts continues beyond the grave.

Since Abraham is not omniscient, how did Abraham know about Moses?

The ministry of Moses and the prophets transpired on earth. Some of the spirits who were now in Abraham's bosom were the very ones who had been under Moses' or the prophets' ministries. This knowledge did not evaporate after they died. Memory persists beyond the grave. This information was stored in either their spirits or souls or both.

It appears that just as men become knowledgeable through fellowshipping with one another on earth, they also become knowledgeable through fellowship and interaction beyond the grave. It would appear that your knowledge widens in relation to the degree and quality of your communion. Therefore, the sphere of your knowledge beyond the grave has a lot to do with the sphere of your interaction. This in turn affects your rate of spiritual development.

The spirit of Abraham did not get transported to the earth to witness the events at Sinai nor was he present at the giving of the Law. He was not omniscient. His knowledge was a product of his interaction.

The saints that have passed on beyond the grave do not suddenly become omniscient. They do not know every detail of every event taking place on the earth. They however know, about the significant spiritual operations on the earth because spirit beings pass on spiritually significant information about the time frame in which they lived and operated during their sojourn on earth. They have insight into the spiritual aspects of everyday life but not the physical activities themselves because the physical aspects are not discussed. Thus Abraham knew about the scriptures that were given to Moses and the message given to the prophets though these ministries were given on the earth centuries after his death.

Locating where leadings originate

All the body parts mentioned in that passage after the burial of the Rich Man are not biological but spiritual.

Through this story, we observe that the inner senses will outlive the outer senses. Note also, that our inner senses are not visible to the outer eye but are in fact eternal. Our outer senses were built as copies of the senses of the spirit man. The spirit man's senses are for contacting the spiritual realm.

The eyes that the rich man lifted up in hell are the eyes of his spirit man. Thus, the spirit man has eyes. We see with our spiritual eye just as we see with our biological eyes. Lazarus also has spiritual fingertips while the rich man has a spiritual tongue. The anatomy of the human spirit is surely not a set of eyes, fingers and a tongue dangling out of nothingness. These parts must be connected in a way that's similar to the arrangement of our biological anatomy. This cements that point that the physical world is a mirror of the spiritual world.

The spirit man's anatomy has fingers, a tongue and eyes as well as a mind, ears and legs. There is a spirit characteristic corresponding to each biological sense in our physical body. You could say that my spiritual neck fills up my physical neck, just like my spiritual tongue and eyes fill up my physical tongue and eyes respectively. My spiritual brain also fills up my natural brain and it is within this spiritual brain that you have the soul.

It is important that we understand this spiritual anatomy because the same place where the utterance of tongues gets generated is where the leadings of the spirit will also flow. The source from which the Holy Spirit speaks to us is within the spiritual mind. God's thoughts originate in your spiritual mind, while your thoughts originate in your natural mind.

Our spiritual senses are not given to us at death. It's just that during the normal course of the day, the majority of us go through our conscious moments totally oblivious of the sensations that our inner senses are broadcasting. The level of distraction in our natural minds usually blocks our consciousness of the spiritual senses. When we dream, these inner senses are more dominant than our outer senses because our conscious minds are not in the way (Job 33:14 - 16). We don't have to sleep in order to sharpen our sensitivity. It is as we allow God's peace rule our hearts that we become aware of our spiritual senses. This is the normal Christian life.

Effects of divine communication

But as it is written: "What has been concealed for ages in a realm inaccessible to the senses; what no human eye could catch a glimpse of, nor man's ear could even hear a whisper of, neither could the inquiring mind decipher the code of that mystery which God has already fully arranged and was ready to reveal to those who love him.".
1 Corinthians 2:9

Paul gives some clues showing how supernatural communion affects man's spiritual anatomy.

God has prepared things for all those that love Him. He is not a hit-and-miss God. Though He has prepared for us, we do not always experience what God has prepared for us. This is because God has so designed us that we cannot be affected by that which does not settle within us. For this reason, the plans of God must be received into our constitution in order to affect us.

The revelations of God produce effects in us. In this instance, God is lamenting that the eyes have not seen, the ears have not heard and the heart has not perceived. This is not the way things are meant to be. He is describing spiritual transfer of data.

For example, if I was having a headache while ministering and God wanted to bring me a Word of knowledge about headaches, He has no problem giving it to me in perception or feeling form. I would likely have a limitation of not being able to distinguish between the ache that God is informing me about and the ache that is pounding my physical body. My physical ache would dull my awareness and cloud my ability to distinguish what God is communicating to me.

In mercy, God would likely transmit that information to me as a form of knowledge.

Therefore, when we do not maintain a healthy body we might be limiting ourselves from fully exploiting the communion we have in God.

When things are normal, once we are exposed to God's Word, the spiritual components of our being react to God's Word in several ways. Usually our eyes begin to see, our ears become better tuned to hearing and our hearts start to perceive afresh.

Our eyes, ears and heart are affected because these energies of sounds, images, feelings and meaning are inherent in God's Word. God's Words contain His sounds, thoughts and feelings, which penetrate into all dimensions of our being.

God's Word transmits sounds, imagery, feelings or perceptions as well as meaning. All that God communicates radiates out with intensity of spiritual sounds, imagery, sensations and meaning.

We all have the faculty for sensing the sights and sounds of God among the myriads of spiritual sensations that are available. However, we are not all equally sensitive to these supernatural effects that God's Word has on us. Some of us are more attuned to the hearing aspect of God's Word without necessarily seeing any images. Then there are others who see the imagery conveyed by God's Word. These tend to hear by seeing. What they see becomes how they "hear". Furthermore, there are yet others who just perceive without being able to tell whether they have heard or seen. They just know that they know, without knowing how they arrived there.

It is God's plan that we grasp the meaning of the things that He has prepared for us. This means that we must progress from the sensation of hearing, seeing and knowing to understanding the meaning or intent of spiritual experiences.

We sharpen our spiritual sense of hearing, seeing and perceiving by continuing to expose ourselves to God's Word. It is the same Word that gives us spiritual sensations that also imparts its meaning. Our human spirit is not satisfied with just seeing or knowing. Our spirit wants to grasp the meaning and intention of that which we have seen and known.

The greatest help that God has given to us to aid us in seeing, knowing and understanding is the born again spirit. It is through our born again spirit that we are able to judge all things correctly.

But God hath revealed them unto us by his Spirit: for the Spirit searcheth
all things, yea, the deep things of God.
1 Corinthians. 2:10

When God reveals things to us, He transfers volumes of information into our lives. This communication is not from the lips of God. There are things that we know all of a sudden that we don't know how we know them nor could so much have been transmitted in split seconds but they are!

It is as we meditate on these transmissions that we search and explore the depths of God. During this process, the full weight of the contents of divine things unfold in us.

God does not communicate through our biological senses but through our spiritual senses. He does this via revelation. Divine revelation is hearing and seeing through the inward senses of the human spirit. It is the spiritual equivalent of hearing and seeing biologically. Divine revelation is from God's Spirit to our spirit, primarily through thoughts and impressions. Revelation imparts insight but it is not directly through the knowledge of any human language itself; rather the meaning and thoughts of God are communicated directly and instantaneously. God does not speak in human language even though we seem to hear God in the language that we are conversant with in our natural mind.

When you appear to hear God speak in a human language, it is because your spirit first understands it in a manner beyond language and then conveys it to your soul in a language that your mind understands. When you hear God speak to you in your vernacular, it is not that He actually verbalised your vernacular. He communicates (spiritually) to your spirit man at a depth too high for the human language to transmit. Your human spirit then steps this down for the benefit of your intellect in your everyday vernacular. Therefore, at the point it registers on your soul, you are convinced that God spoke your vernacular.

Divine revelation is an impartation of experience and knowledge. It is like data exchange between two mobile phones, except that while this mobile illustration explains the idea of the flow of facts, it does not show the transfer of the full experience and sensations involved with divine revelation.

God is a revealing God

Revelation carries the idea of unveiling or showing that which was previously hidden. Though it is not always visual, it is obvious that the visual component is very strong. The spirit sends and receives spiritual impulses in image form.

For what man knoweth the things of a man, save the spirit of man which is in him? even so the things of God knoweth no man, but the Spirit of God.
1 Corinthians 2:11

The spirit of man possesses a spiritual intellect that is capable of knowing things by discerning them spiritually. This spiritual discerning is the realm of perceptions and feelings. It is a depth of comprehension that is beyond that which can be explained through the intellect of the soul.

There are whole experiences that God gives to us that we need to spiritually discern. We become better at discerning these things as we speak God's Word in our understanding and speak spiritual mysteries in other tongues. We must learn to spend time in the Word and learn to obey our recreated spirit as the Holy Ghost teaches us about spiritual things.

24x7 Sensitivity

G od yearns to speak to man in man's wakeful moments.

However prior to Jesus making the New Birth available, God mostly waited for man to fall asleep before He could get His messages to man (Job 33:14-15).

We see this in the famous Christmas story.

> *Now the birth of Jesus Christ was on this wise: When as his mother Mary was espoused to Joseph, before they came together, she was found with child of the Holy Ghost. Then Joseph her husband, being a just man, and not willing to make her a public example, was minded to put her away privily. But while he thought on these things, behold, the angel of the LORD appeared unto him in a dream, saying, Joseph, thou son of David, fear not to take unto thee Mary thy wife: for that which is conceived in her is of the Holy Ghost.*
> *Matthew 1:18-20*

Joseph was traumatised when Mary told him that she was supernaturally pregnant (Is there a man who wouldn't be?). Her pregnancy was a spectacular working of God. Joseph's mind could not fathom such a thing. That kind of pregnancy was unknown in human experience. It was contrary to the known process for conception and pregnancy. Joseph had decided to end their engagement in a way that wouldn't put Mary to shame. Joseph was thinking about his plan to divorce Mary. We do not know whether Joseph was thinking on the Isaiah 7 prophecy about the virgin that shall be with child.

It was in his sleep that the angel appeared to Joseph in a dream to give him counsel from God that confirmed the virgin conception to him. God likely used Isaiah's prophecy to assure Joseph.

Instruction in the night seasons

I will bless the LORD, who hath given me counsel: my reins also instruct me in the night seasons.
Psalm 16:7

The Psalmist speaks of instruction coming in the night seasons.

Now a thing was secretly brought to me, and mine ear received a little thereof. In thoughts from the visions of the night, when deep sleep falleth on men,
Job 4:12-13

Notice that Job also talked of secrets coming through visions of the night when men drift into deep sleep.

God is a spirit. He communicates spiritually but many times we do not perceive what He is transmitting to us partly because we expect Him to communicate with us through our physical senses. Our failure to appreciate that we are spirit beings just as God is a spirit being is a great hindrance to receiving what God is communicating to us. God is always talking. The challenge is on our side of the fence.

If we understand the why of this night-time communion we are able to perceive that communion strongly during our wakeful moments. I don't want to wait until night before I get these downloads.

Resistance through the carnal mind

For to be carnally minded is death; but to be spiritually minded is life and peace. 7 Because the carnal mind is enmity against God: for it is not subject to the law of God, neither indeed can be.
Romans 8:6

The carnal mind is the bank where the counsel as well as the thoughts of the flesh takes residence. It is where the wrong thoughts, imagination and strongholds are stored and processed. It acts as a signal station that cancels out those signals that agree with God. This is the mind that governs the natural man. This carnal mind is the dominant consciousness in the natural man. This is also what governs the walk of the born again man who walks in the flesh.

The chief characteristic of the carnal mind is that it is not subject to the laws of God. Thus in our wakeful moments, the carnal mind successfully resists the transmissions that God is sending our way. It prevents the divine transmissions through the human spirit from getting into the heart, by erecting a thick wall between the soul and the spirit.

The spirit-to-spirit transmissions of God register in the human spirit but it does not penetrate into the consciousness of the carnal-minded man. The signals of God do not register on our consciousness because the carnal mind neutralises it through anxieties cares and worries.

The carnal mind is enmity against God and is not subject to God. Notice that the bible says, "neither indeed can it be". We understand by this that it is impossible for the carnal mind to receive from God! This is the singular greatest reason why God ends up talking to man in the night-time. It is not that God gets stronger as the day wears on until He is at maximum strength at night. That cannot be the case since at any point in time some part of the earth is experiencing night and some other part is experiencing daylight. Thus night is not global. The whole earth does not experience night at once. God is not strong for half of the earth and weak for the other.

The reason why God communicates with man at night more than at any other time of the day is because of the way the carnal mind functions. The ability of the carnal mind to block out God's signals to us fluctuates. The implication is that the carnal mind is not as effective in blocking out the transmissions of God at night as it is during the day. The reason for this characteristic is not because the night-time is a more spiritual time. It is that way because the night-time is when men sleep. If a man works night shifts and sleeps during the day, then his "night-time" is during the day when he sleeps.

God waits until the carnal mind is at its lowest strength, which coincides with when we are asleep. He then drops His counsel into the heart of man.

The carnal mind is at its lowest strength when we are asleep because at that time we are doing little talking. It is with our words that we release the power of life and death (Prov. 18:20). Spoken words give life to thoughts. While we are asleep, thoughts exist but in the absence of our words their ability to affect us is greatly limited. When men release the power of death through their words, it creates a spiritual blanket or fog that makes spiritual things indistinct. This is the carnal mind at its lethal worst.

Since a large portion of the population in a particular geography sleep at about the same time, the cumulative spiritual power released through spoken words is weakest at night when people are asleep. This means that satan's ability to rule through the cumulative of men voicing their thoughts is also greatly limited.

Job gives an excellent description of the experience of fallen man.

> *For God speaketh once, yea twice, yet man perceiveth it not.15 In a dream, in a vision of the night, when deep sleep falleth upon men, in slumberings upon the bed; Then he openeth the ears of men, and sealeth their instruction, That he may withdraw man from his purpose, and hide pride from man*
> *Job 33:14-17*

In the unsaved man, the carnal mind is an extension of the carnal nature of a dead spirit. The spirit and the mind fully agree to mount up a wall that resists the things of God. Natural man is blind and deaf to God. All the thoughts that the unsaved considers are carnal. Therefore, the resistance projected from his soul against God is extremely strong. Their consciousness is powered fully by the carnal mind, which conforms the man to the world system.

Renewing the mind

And be not conformed to this world: but be ye transformed by the renewing of your mind, that ye may prove what is that good, and acceptable, and perfect, will of God.
Romans 12:2

God instructs the born again one to be transformed by the renewing of the mind. By this, God is not asking that we renovate or improve on the carnal mind for God wants no part of the carnal mind whatsoever. He doesn't want to renovate it.

When a man receives eternal life, he has access to another mind in his reborn spirit. This mind agrees with God, for it is of the spirit that is born of God. God wants us to switch our consciousness from the carnal mind and its lusts to the mind of the new man as we feed on God's Word.

Over a period of time, as we become more conscious of the Word, and the light of God's Word shines into our soul, the effect of the resistance mounted by the carnal mind diminishes. We become more Word-and-spirit conscious throughout the day. This way, even in our waking moments, we can perceive, receive and correctly interpret God's communication to us. We no longer have to go to bed in order for God to get through to us.

For God, who commanded the light to shine out of darkness, hath shined in our hearts, to give the light of the knowledge of the glory of God in the face of Jesus Christ.
2 Corinthians 4:6

The New Birth is God giving light to our hearts by imparting His life into our spirits.

The spirit of the man who is not born again abides in spiritual death and generates darkness since that spirit is separate from the life of God. In the born again man, the reborn spirit generates excellent thoughts filled with light. This is how God causes His light to shine out of our reborn spirit into our hearts. He does this in every born again one. However, not every born again one takes advantage of this. If we keep embracing the thoughts coming from the carnal mind, we become dull to the light of life shinning out of our spirits. These thoughts that we embrace become satan's inroad, through which he enforces darkness (See Eph. 4:17-18). Thus we would find it harder to perceive what God is saying in that area. A Christian that only hears from God in his sleep is effectively functioning like the world. He is little esteeming the Word, ignoring the light that God is shining into his heart and not using his privileges in Christ Jesus. He is an infant. God wants the infants to grow up so that our nurseries can nurture real spiritual babies.

Words, power and thoughts

Be careful for nothing; but in every thing by prayer and supplication with thanksgiving let your requests be made known unto God. And the peace of God, which passeth all understanding, shall keep your hearts and minds through Christ Jesus. Finally, brethren, whatsoever things are true, whatsoever things are honest, whatsoever things are just, whatsoever things are pure, whatsoever things are lovely, whatsoever things are of good report; if there be any virtue, and if there be any praise, think on these things.
Philippians 4:6-8

Praying correctly and effectively supplies spiritual power. We follow up on our prayer by releasing this available power **through spoken words.**

Reasoning carnally introduces a lot of anxiety into the heart. If we follow up on our prayer with anxiety, it consumes and drains away spiritual power. Anxiety in the heart cancels out God's signals. When we speak unbelief, we block out the power of God in our spirit. When God's Word is not coming out of our mouths anxiety flows from the flesh and the environment and overwhelms our hearts and clouds our spiritual discernment. People who voice their anxieties enforce a lot of cancellation in their heart by their mouth for death and life are in the power of the tongue.

After we have prayed the Word of God, the peace of God is released from our spirits to our souls. This is one way that the peace of God comes into our minds from our spirits. Peace guards the mind and heart against anxiety.

We keep and perfect God's peace in our hearts by focusing our minds on the Word of God (Isaiah 26:3). The thoughts that persist in our soul will direct and distribute the power that had been supplied through prayer and released through words.

God uses His Word coming out of our mouths to lead us (Prov. 3:6). The Word of God spoken out of our mouths, then causes the peace of God to guard our hearts and we become more sensitive to God's direction.

Spiritual power is not released through thoughts but through spoken words. Yet it is particularly important that we fill our thoughts with God's Word after we have spoken in prayer. This is because we use our thoughts to direct this power into our souls, until the correct actions are birthed.

Praying the scriptures and speaking in other tongues builds us up in edification, which we then speak out with our mouths, channel with our thoughts, until we operate in ways that cause us to perceive God's leadings distinctly. Our words release spiritual power and our thoughts broadcast that power into our souls and our environment.

Speaking God's Word out of our own mouths releases the power of God resident in our spirits out through our souls into our thoughts and our atmosphere.

First we pray the Word, and then we fill our thoughts with God's Word after which those thoughts birth right actions.

If we operate this way long enough, others can walk into our presence and reap the fruit of peace in our lives. It would be easier for them to yield to God's peace when they are around us. This is not their level. They are just reaping the fruits of associating with us.

There are many other people in our world who are speaking a lot of unbelief and following it up with thinking thoughts that are contrary to God's Word. They believe wrong, think wrong and act wrong actions. This deadly combination gives satan inroads through which he steals their confidence and robs them of peace. Such people are projecting confusion wherever they go as they voice their beliefs. They are acting as satan's broadcast station through which he amplifies his wrong thoughts in much the same way that masts and repeaters boost radio signals making it easy for distant radios to pick up the station's signals. People worry around them with ease. There is no struggle.

Why is satan so effective?

And we know that we are of God, and the whole world lieth in wickedness.
1 John 5:19

The whole world is in the grip of the wicked one.

The spirit of the sinner is full of spiritual death. This death is poured out of their hearts through their mouths. This forms a shield of unbelief that blocks out the light of God's Word in their own hearts (see 2 Cor. 4:3). There is a cumulative effect when the power released through many men is combined to form thick barriers enforced through beliefs and spoken words. Men find it harder to yield to the truth of God. Through their beliefs, thoughts and actions men supply the power with which satan rules in darkness. Satan uses these men like booster stations to amplify the wrong thoughts that they give voice to. The words of these men are used to assault their minds, as well as the minds of others with thoughts. If others do not protect their minds by focusing it on God's Word, they'll get distracted from God's Word.

For the weapons of our warfare are not carnal, but mighty through God to the pulling down of strong holds; Casting down imaginations, and every high thing that exalteth itself against the knowledge of God, and bringing into captivity every thought to the obedience of Christ;
2 Corinthians.10:4-5

Thoughts, imaginations and strongholds are projected around the world in much the same way that radio signals bounce round the earth through various repeaters, amplifiers and boosters. Spiritually speaking, human beings function as repeaters and power stations allowing the footprint of darkness cover large portions of the earth. It is that way because men yield that much to satan's wiles and tricks. The enemy does not come against us with power but with thoughts and ideas.

There are thoughts everywhere on this earth. They are not powerful until men rebroadcast them through their words.

Certainly these thoughts have little power over you if you will not accept them. Once you accept a thought through your will, it develops into imaginations, which grow up into strongholds that exalt themselves against the knowledge of God's Word!

This is not isolated to just a few people. The whole world walks in the vanity of their minds. Apparently, Christians can also operate this way. We don't have to walk in a vain mind, if we will yield to the nature of God within us. The spiritual mind brings us the revelations and transmissions of God.

If through our wills, we walk in the vanity of our minds, we end up with strongholds, which drain spiritual power from us and make it available to satan. He has no power of his own but uses the power of those who yield to his thoughts.

When we accept these thoughts they drain away the power that we have generated in prayer. This prevents peace from flowing out into our soul. Our soul is pulling confusion into our heart instead of pulling peace from our human spirit.

After Mary had told Joseph about her incredible pregnancy, his mind could not compute it. It was contrary to natural thinking. It was much easier to believe that Mary had been unfaithful. Most people would reason that way. They think they are street smart. It was Joseph's carnal mind that prevented him from hearing God assure him that Mary's tale was in line with prophecy and that it was of God. Joseph's carnal mind overrode everything else he might have learnt from Isaiah about the sign of the virgin who was to be with child. The carnal mind blocked out light in that area.

God's dealing with Mary did not confuse Joseph for God is not the author of confusion. Carnal reasoning filled Joseph with confusion and caused him to stumble in the dark. He was not hardened against God's Word; it's just that the carnal mind is a formidable foe. Since he was not thinking the Word, he was powerless against confusion flowing from his carnal mind.

Joseph was not born again. There was little God could do but wait. God bid His time until Joseph went to bed, by which time the resistance of the carnal mind would be subdued.

Since God works with His Word, it is likely that God got through to Joseph by causing him to hear or see Isaiah 7:14 in his dream. If you fill your mind with God's Word, it is easier for God to get through to you.

The born again Christian will know these things firstly by an inward witness, which helps us know that the scripture quoted applies in the given situation. Your spirit's inward witness and the Word effectively mean you have at least two witnesses. This establishes the matter (2 Cor. 13:1). This witness is accompanied by peace. As we pay attention to it, this becomes joy. Peace is the umpire in these matters. It is your responsibility to sense that peace and allow it make the call.

Sometimes God can't get across through a dream

However God is not always able to get through to man through a dream. King Saul illustrates this.

The will of man is the tunnel between the spirit and the mind. A will submitted to God's Word causes light from the spirit or the Word to flood the mind and cut away the resistance of the carnal mind.

Where the will is set against the Word, no light flows through in that area.

For rebellion is as the sin of witchcraft, and stubbornness is as iniquity and idolatry. Because thou hast rejected the word of the LORD, he hath also rejected thee from being king.
1 Samuel 15:23

King Saul's real trouble was that he had rejected God's Word.

Pride is the absence of light. We can say that pride prevents the entrance of the light of God's Word.

And Samuel said to Saul, Why hast thou disquieted me, to bring me up? And Saul answered, I am sore distressed; for the Philistines make war against me, and God is departed from me, and answereth me no more, neither by prophets, nor by dreams: therefore I have called thee, that thou mayest make known unto me what I shall do.
1 Samuel 28:15

The pride in Saul's heart thickened the barrier between the spirit realm and his mind, to the point where even in his dream life he could not perceive God's warnings. God did not change towards Saul, it was Saul that hardened towards God. His bitterness choked that tunnel through which spirit-to-mind communion occurred. He locked himself out by his wilful pride, which blinded him to the light of God. The carnal mind was operating at full strength in Saul.

The light of the body is the eye: therefore when thine eye is single, thy whole body also is full of light; but when thine eye is evil, thy body also is full of darkness. Take heed therefore that the light which is in thee be not darkness.
Luke 11:34-35

Saul's eye, which is the lamp of his body, was absorbing darkness while shutting out the light of God's Word. This left him no choice but to be taken captive by and to operate fully in the carnal mind. The entrance of the Word usually gives light but the Word had no entrance to his darkened mind. In his own case, he wilfully rejected God's Word.

In those areas, where the Word had no access to Saul's mind, the carnal mind exerted tremendous blinding power. This caused him to walk in darkness in those areas. His mental faculties became satan's broadcast station into the world. In those areas, he could not hear God. If God attempted to get revelation to Saul in that area in his wakeful or sleeping moments that revelation was hid from him by the blindness that was in his heart in that area.

Some people are blind in a few areas; therefore, the resistance mounted through the carnal mind is not as extensive as it is in others who have large areas of their lives where they resist God's Word. Their hearts function as stronger transmission stations projecting darkness and blocking out light.

Feast on God's Word by praying in tongues, and saying and thinking the Word long enough until it dismantles the thick barrier between spirit and soul. This will cause peace to flood the heart and protect it all day.

The Peculiarities of Joseph's Dreams

Joseph's is the name that comes up, when dreams are discussed in the bible. His dreams were recorded as early as his seventeenth birthday (Gen 37:2).

In the Old Testament, it is kings or prophets that dream those dreams that prove significant to the destinies of communities, kingdoms and nations. What is peculiar about Joseph is that when he dreamt his dreams, he was neither a prophet nor a king. Notwithstanding his dreams would prove significant to the destiny of Israel.

Also, we do not find in any of them expressions like,

"And the angel of the Lord said to Joseph in a dream"

"And God appeared to Joseph in a dream saying"

The bible neither records Joseph seeing visions like Abraham, Isaac and Jacob nor does it say that he heard any distinct, direct word from God. In fact Joseph is never referred to as a prophet anywhere in the bible.

His dreams are therefore personal dreams with a twist, in that Joseph understood them to be so significant they'd affect the destiny of the whole nation.

Do not interpretations belong to God?

And they said unto him, We have dreamed a dream, and there is no interpreter of it. And Joseph said unto them, Do not interpretations belong to God? tell me them, I pray you.
Genesis 40:8

When these dreamers said there was no interpreter, they were saying there was no one to solve their problem. The Hebrew word translated interpreter here means to solve a problem.

Pharaoh used the same word in his interaction with Joseph,

And Pharaoh said unto Joseph, I have dreamed a dream, and there is none that can interpret it: and I have heard say of thee, that thou canst understand a dream to interpret it.
Genesis 41:15

When Pharaoh said there was no one to interpret, he was saying that though he had seen something in his dream, there was no one to solve his problem of not understanding what he had observed in his dream.

Notice that interpretation and understanding are related. You interpret in order to communicate understanding of that which has been seen or heard.

This dream came to them. They did not generate it. It was a God-given dream. While God-given dreams play out within man, they are not of human origin.

Joseph was not saying that God gives the interpretation to all dreams. He was stating the important fact that God gives the interpretation of God-given dreams.

A quality of God-given dreams is that God, the giver, knows the meaning of the dream. If the interpretation of a dream is wrong, then the dream is not understood. You don't guess the meaning of a God-given dream. You receive its meaning from God just as you received the dream in the first instance!

The interpretation of a dream conveys to the mind of the dreamer, the mind of the one who gave the dream to the dreamer. This is also true of the interpretation of tongues or a spiritual vision.

The interpretation of a God-given dream conveys the mind of God to the mind of the dreamer so that the dreamer can solve the problem of not understanding the dream that God had given him.

Pharaoh's officials, who were the dreamers, had a problem in that they did not know the meaning of the dreams they had received, until aided by another who was not necessarily the one that dreamt. This idea of not understanding God-given dreams is characteristic of sinners. In the bible there is no instance where a saint did not know the meaning of a God-given dream.

Observe closely that the chief baker was present when Joseph interpreted the butler's dream (see Gen. 40:16). Until Joseph interpreted that dream, the baker was as confused as the butler. They each could have jumped to fanciful conclusions but did not. Joseph was the one that received the interpretation from God. They received their understanding from Joseph.

Many people excel at dreaming but they are however poor at interpreting it. A good dreamer does not make a good interpreter. The ability to dream is universal but the ability to interpret is less so. Furthermore, gaining understanding from the interpretation of dreams is an acquired and learned skill developed over time. Pharaoh did not celebrate those that knew how to dream. He was awed by Joseph's ability to convey the meaning of another person's dream.

Seeing a spiritual sign and correctly interpreting it are two different things.

A fellow could see specific words in his dream, this does not mean he understands what he has seen. He might know the translation. This doesn't mean he understands it. A word can be accurately translated but poorly interpreted. Everyone saw the finger writing on the wall in Daniel's day (see Daniel 5:4-28). Today, we know that the words written on the wall were "MENE, MENE, TEKEL, UPHARSIN". If you were an expert in ancient languages you might find that the translation of each word was not hard. Literally, the translation is number, weigh and divide. You wouldn't know the meaning of the words by knowing what each word meant. No one understood the message contained in those words except Daniel who was given the interpretation by God.

Don't assume interpretations

After listening to his dream, collectively, Joseph's brothers' Interpretation was - thou shall reign over us. This was their collective interpretation of what they thought the dream meant. This was not necessarily the God-given interpretation.

Their Sheaves were bowing to Joseph's in Joseph's dream.

They assumed that just by listening to a dream they understood its meaning. Perhaps the brothers should have asked Joseph what he perceived the meaning to be. It was his dream and not theirs. They likely had the translation but not the interpretation.

When Joseph started relaying his dreams as a teenager, his brothers assumed that they knew the general meaning of his dreams. They assumed them to be the active mind of a teenager who had grand ideas about his own importance for Jacob had given Joseph preferential treatment. They did not take the dreams to be a message from God. It is peculiar that Joseph's brothers did not take his dreams seriously because generally in the Old Testament dreams were taken seriously. However, Jacob secretly kept those dreams in his heart (see Gen 37:11). Joseph's dreams were the first recorded dreams in the bible that were not taken seriously.

Interestingly, in Joseph's life, his dreams were always double. He dreamt two dreams, Pharaoh dreamt two dreams and we could combine the Chief Baker and Butler's dreams as two.

The recurring theme in Joseph's dreams is that of bowing. In the first, the sheaves of others bowed down to his and in the second, the sun, moon and the eleven stars bowed down to him. The second dream that included the sun and moon expanded on the first in which only his brothers were in view. Joseph had the same dream twice, thus showing the certainty of its message.

Joseph's treatment in the hand of his brethren is a figure of Christ's treatment when He was rejected as the corner stone, was put to death and yet rose up as Lord of all.

His brothers were troubled by the fact that they bowed to him in his dreams. They interpreted this in terms of power therefore they envied him more. We know that ten of his brothers literally all bowed to him later when he was ruling in Egypt (see Gen 42:6). It was at this time that Joseph remembered his dreams. Interestingly there is no bible record that Benjamin bowed before Joseph. Also there is no record of Jacob, Joseph's mum or step mum bowing before Joseph although in one of his earlier dreams, the sun and moon bowed before him. The intention behind Joseph's dreams was that through Joseph's exaltation, the knowledge of God would increase among the heathen.

Joseph's ability to interpret dreams was going to be more crucial in bringing about his exaltation than his ability to dream. Through the exercise of that gift of interpretation, God used Joseph at age 30 to save the known world from death. Egypt owed him. The world was indebted to him (see Gen 41:57). In fact, all Egypt bowed to Joseph before any of his brothers ever did. It was as a result of his excellent interpretation and application that Pharaoh and his court ended up knowing about the Spirit of God (See Gen. 41:38). Thus the known world got to know about God starting from Egypt! I am convinced that God's true reason for Joseph's life was that through Joseph, the knowledge of God would increase upon the earth. God's agenda was not about the power play between him and his brothers. It was the mercy of God rescuing man from the effects of Adam's fall. The whole world would thank him and be indebted to him and his God.

It is worthy of note that the seven years of famine did not come from God. The intense famine was a calamity that would have resulted in the loss of many innocent lives. That famine was a function of the curse that came from satan, through Adam's fall, into the earth.

Pharaoh's dreams did not cause the years of famine or plenty. There would have been plenty and scarcity whether Pharaoh dreamt or not. God helped Pharaoh plan properly. Scarcity and plenty come in cycles in this imperfect world, we simply get better at knowing how to use it to optimise our benefit. It is interesting that God, through Joseph, did not tell Pharaoh to offer sacrifices in order that there might be no years of scarcity.

Joseph's brothers could have interpreted bowing as signifying their gratitude to Joseph. In other words, they could have taken it to mean that Joseph saw ahead that they would be grateful to him that God preserved Jacob's people through Joseph finding favour in Egypt.

We know from the bible that bowing down can be the expression of a thankful heart (Gen 24:26-52 & Gen 33:3).

Joseph's brothers interpreted his dream as reflecting the outcome of a power tussle. Their envy caused them to consider murder. They did not like the dream or the dreamer because of the wrong interpretation they had put on his dreams. Their envy coloured their interpretation. It prevented them from seeing the bigger picture.

Interpreting dreams is not to be taken lightly. Trying to act on a dream without renewing your mind to God's Word often results in tragedy.

Joseph is also the only one who was to be killed because of his dreams (Gen 37:20).

We are not told that Joseph interpreted his own dreams at the beginning although it is implied that he knew the meaning.
About thirteen years later, he shows his understanding of the dream and shared his views with his brothers. He saw himself as a saviour and not as their ruler (Gen. 45:5-8). Their bowing down would therefore indicate that they acknowledged that God was using him and they were grateful. It is likely that Joseph himself came to see the intent of his dreams when he forgave his brothers and let go of any resentment that he had felt towards them before the seven years of famine started (Gen 41:51).

And he said unto them, Hear, I pray you, this dream which I have dreamed: For, behold, we were binding sheaves in the field, and, lo, my sheaf arose, and also stood upright; and, behold, your sheaves stood round about, and made obeisance to my sheaf. And his brethren said to him, Shalt thou indeed reign over us? or shalt thou indeed have dominion over us? And they hated him yet the more for his dreams, and for his words. And he dreamed yet another dream, and told it his brethren, and said, Behold, I have dreamed a dream more; and, behold, the sun and the moon and the eleven stars made obeisance to me. And he told it to his father, and to his brethren: and his father rebuked him, and said unto him, What is this dream that thou hast dreamed? Shall I and thy mother and thy brethren indeed come to bow down ourselves to thee to the earth?
Genesis 37:6-10

All of Joseph's dreams were about himself, in the same way the overwhelming majority of your dreams are about you.

Joseph relayed his dream to his own inner circle but did not tell anyone its meaning. We do not know if at that time he knew the meaning. He likely did. He told the dream but kept the meaning to himself.

It is possible that Joseph told the dream because he hoped his brothers would see him as a gracious help in the days ahead. Instead of seeing him as a help, they saw him as one who wanted to lord it over them.

The dreams did not give him details about where he would rule, when he would rule, how it would come about or whether he would be in prison. We look to God for those kinds of details. Details tend to mature over a lifetime of walking with God. God gives us enough detail so we can walk by faith and not by sight.

Joseph was not the first to dream but he is the first one that demonstrates the bible principle that dreams and spiritual experiences are to be interpreted. They cannot always be taken at face value. Much damage is done when people ignore this principle.

Joseph is one of the few people who dreamt of the distant future in the bible. He dreamt about his future. He is the first man in the bible with a distinct God-given gift for interpreting the dream of others.

We notice that all the people whose dreams he interpreted were sinners as well as people of influence. None of them was a saint. It is noteworthy that in the bible, we don't find any saint, whether in the Old Testament or in the New Testament, approaching another person in order to receive the interpretation of their dreams. The norm is that once a saint has a God-given dream, that saint would eventually also have the interpretation for God is a revealing God.

Interpretation of the Chief Butler's dream

Joseph's interpretation of Pharaoh's Butler's dream is worthy of study.

And the chief butler told his dream to Joseph, and said to him, In my dream, behold, a vine was before me; And in the vine were three branches: and it was as though it budded, and her blossoms shot forth; and the clusters thereof brought forth ripe grapes: And Pharaoh's cup was in my hand: and I took the grapes, and pressed them into Pharaoh's cup, and I gave the cup into Pharaoh's hand. And Joseph said unto him, This is the interpretation of it: The three branches are three days: Yet within three days shall Pharaoh lift up thine head, and restore thee unto thy place: and thou shalt deliver Pharaoh's cup into his hand, after the former manner when thou wast his butler.

Genesis 40:9-13

The butler is like a chief cupbearer to Pharaoh; therefore holding Pharaoh's cup in his hands is a good thing. Pressing grapes into cups would represent his job as Pharaoh's go-to person for wine. The dream was saying something good about the restoration of his job. Since that which buds is bringing forth fresh life, it would appear that there was coming new lease of life to the butler's service to Pharaoh.

Notice that instead of dreaming of the passage of three days, the Butler had seen it in parable form as the three branches in his dream. Each branch represented a day. Therefore, the three branches represented three days. So we see that in dreams, the passage of time does not show itself as time, watches or clocks necessarily.

The Butler's dream told the Butler what was happening in the immediate future in the Butler's life – within three days.

We also notice that all the images in the Butler's dream had a positive slant to them. This was going to be a good dream. Joseph concluded that the Butler was going to be restored to his role as Pharaoh's chief Butler.

The Butler was dreaming about himself.

Notice that Joseph's interpretation showed that the Butler's dream covered the same sphere and level of operation as the Butler. There is an important point to note here. The interpretation of the Butler's dream showed that his dream had a bearing to where he was in life. The sphere of the Butler's operation was to stand in the presence of Pharaoh. Since the Butler's sphere of operation was not international, the dream and its interpretation would not be international.

If you are reading this book, you are not the Butler and you don't serve the Pharaoh of Egypt. Therefore, it would be theatrical for God to show you a vision in which you were squeezing juice into Pharaoh's cup. Squeezing juice into cups does not universally mean jobs. That is not a universal principle. It had a specific meaning, given the context of the Butler's life.

The Butler was sad after his dream mainly because he did not know how to interpret his own dream. His dream carried the prophecy of his release and restoration to high office but his ignorance kept him depressed.

A person who is untrained in the Word, who is not spirit-conscious and whose mind is not being renewed could have the best dream with the best message in the world but put a wrong interpretation on it. We do not use our emotional state to judge whether we have had a bad dream.

Interpretation of the Chief Baker's dream

When the chief baker saw that the interpretation was good, he said unto Joseph, I also was in my dream, and, behold, I had three white baskets on my head: And in the uppermost basket there was of all manner of bakemeats for Pharaoh; and the birds did eat them out of the basket upon my head. And Joseph answered and said, This is the interpretation thereof: The three baskets are three days: Yet within three days shall Pharaoh lift up thy head from off thee, and shall hang thee on a tree; and the birds shall eat thy flesh from off thee.
Genesis 40:16-19

Apparently the Baker listened in on Joseph's brilliant interpretation of the Butler's dream therefore he also wanted his own dream interpreted.

It would appear that the dreams that involved Joseph in the bible started from the relatively simple to the increasingly complex. The Baker's dream was more complex. It was a dream about the death of the dreamer. Joseph did not manufacture a politically correct interpretation in order to please the Baker. Thank God His life within gives us His reputation for integrity. The love of money, as well as fear, cloud our ability to give clear interpretations.

The Baker saw birds eating the bakeries meant for Pharaoh out of the basket on the baker's head. It does not seem right that birds of the air should eat Pharaoh's food, does it? The birds eating Pharaoh's pastries was not cool. In all, his dream meant that in three days he was going to become food for the vultures that feed off a dead carcass. He had dreamt of his own death.

The Baker had dreamt of his own death and yet in that dream, he did not actually see himself at his funeral, in a fainting spell or a mortuary. His death had been conveyed to him in symbolic language. This means that most dreams that people dream where they see their own death has nothing to do with physical death. It mostly refers to something else. Physical death is often not conveyed as death but as something more symbolic.

In the Baker's dream, each basket represented a day. Therefore, the three baskets represented three days. The passage of time did not show itself as watches or clocks necessarily.

In an unusual twist, it does not look like Pharaoh's Baker could do anything about the death. Death appeared inevitable in his case. A saint understands that these things are conditional even if the condition is not stated. As we repent and act on the Word of God, we are able to avert outcomes that would otherwise have looked like they were destined to happen.

Once again we notice that the Baker was dreaming about himself.

Time frame

The dreams of the Butler and Baker show us that we can gain insight into timeframes involved in dreams by taking note of the numbers that stood out to us within the dream or as we recall it afterwards.

Images don't always mean the same thing

If the Baker later became Pharaoh's Butler, his dreams will

change. If God wanted to tell him about his job, God would no longer use the symbol of bread. Bread is not what he now does; it represents what he used to do. In other words, images don't have a fixed meaning but change according to where we are in our walk. It is not formulaic.

They dreamed a dream both of them

And they dreamed a dream both of them, each man his dream in one night, each man according to the interpretation of his dream, the butler and the baker of the king of Egypt, which were bound in the prison.
Genesis 40:5

Where the KJV says, "they dreamed a dream both of them", our English bible usually states it somewhat differently as:

The two of them dreamt dreams.

Some scholars point out that if we stay grammatically true to Hebrew, the correct rendering is:

They dreamt the dream of both of them.

Reading it as, "The two of them dreamt dreams", would mean that each official dreamt his dream. This is simple to grasp and it is likely the conclusion to be reached by a straightforward, casual reading of the verse. Whereas, "They dreamt the dream of both of them", would imply that this is an instance of shared dreams. In other words, each of these officials dreamt their own dream as well as the dream of the other official!

We notice that while Pharaoh had dreams of prophetic significance, the Butler and the Baker only dreamt about personal concerns relating to their jobs and welfare. You dream within your sphere our influence.

Pharaoh

And Pharaoh said unto Joseph, In my dream, behold, I stood upon the bank of the river: And, behold, there came up out of the river seven kine, fatfleshed and well favoured; and they fed in a meadow: And, behold, seven other kine came up after them, poor and very ill favoured and leanfleshed, such as I never saw in all the land of Egypt for badness: And the lean and the ill favoured kine did eat up the first seven fat kine: And when they had eaten them up, it could not be known that they had eaten them; but they were still ill favoured, as at the beginning. So I awoke. And I saw in my dream, and, behold, seven ears came up in one stalk, full and good: And, behold, seven ears, withered, thin, and blasted with the east wind, sprung up after them: And the thin ears devoured the seven good ears: and I told this unto the magicians; but there was none that could declare it to me. And Joseph said unto Pharaoh, The dream of Pharaoh is one: God hath shewed Pharaoh what he is about to do.
Genesis 41:17-25

This chapter opens with the statement, "When two full years had passed". Hebrew scholars tell us that this should be rendered 'after two years of days'. This would mean that Pharaoh had this dream on a specific day that was exactly two years after the cupbearer had been released and restored to his position. Thus Pharaoh dreamt this significant dream on his birthday. Having that kind of dream on his birthday must have troubled the king.

All of Joseph's spiritual development led to that moment when he was ushered into Pharaoh's presence to interpret Pharaoh's dream.

Pharaoh had a significant God-given dream, woke up and drifted off into sleep again and dreamt another equally significant one afterwards. That dream was going to determine the physical livelihood of a significant portion of most of the civilised world at that time. Mishandling it would have dire consequences.

This is the first dream in the bible where the dreamer is not dreaming about himself. He is dreaming about others. We notice that this is a king, a leader of the people.

We learn from this that God would not give you a dream that you were powerless to influence. Pharaoh was given that dream because he could do something on that scale.

Joseph's dream in which he saw the standing sheaves bears a strong resemblance to Pharaoh's dream about the ears of corn. In all likelihood, this was the anchor that Joseph used to know the interpretation of the dream and more importantly, the part that he was to play in its fulfilment. Joseph would be that person who would succeed at gathering grain when failure looked imminent.

Pharaoh's dream is also the first dream in the bible that the dreamer could not interpret. The dreamer is not a saint but the interpreter is one. Therefore, the things that confuse the heathen should not confound the people of God. As Christians we do not go around seeking someone to interpret our own dream. Our Joseph is within us. The combination of the recreated spirit, the Holy Spirit, meditating on the Word and praying in tongues will work together to remove the burden of not knowing the meaning of God-given dreams.

The other thing to note is that some spiritual things become clearer in the presence of certain individuals who are going to contribute to its fulfilment. There are some interpretations that become more real to us as we walk in the light and open ourselves up to meet the people that God is linking us with. The dots get arranged piece-by-piece until a clear picture emerges.

What was God about to do?

Joseph acknowledged that an unsaved king was given a prophetic dream concerning what was God about to do (Gen. 41:25).

How do we interpret that statement from Joseph about what God was about to do? We must harmonize it with our understanding of God's nature. God had not given those seven years of famine. That famine was a function of the curse that came from satan, through Adam into the earth. God's part in the whole episode was to warn Pharaoh and to send Joseph with the interpretation as well as the wisdom to avert satan's trap.

In this dream, Pharaoh saw himself standing by the banks of the Nile. Joseph said that though Pharaoh had dreamt two dreams, both dreams were one and the same, in that they conveyed the same message.

In that dream, the fat cows came out of the Nile and the thin cows ate the fat cows.

In real life, cows don't come out of rivers nor are they excellent swimmers. Moreover, cows are not carnivorous. So what's with this idea of one cow eating the other?

The imagery used within the dream is not true to nature or experience.

The stalks of grain and the fat cows are images that represent the same thing. The dream is not about stalks of grain or cows.

Stalks of grain would signify fruitful harvest.

The 7 good heads of corn and the fat cows represented the same thing. They represented 7 years of economic boom.

The 7 sickly heads of corn and the thin cows represented the same thing. They represented 7 years of economic burst.

Collectively, it means that there would be seven years of economic boom followed by another seven years where everything goes bust. This earth goes in cycles of abundance and lack. Pharaoh's dream did not initiate any of this. Pharaoh could not change the earth but he could affect his own readiness. God had given Pharaoh insight so he could patiently plan. Economic forces still work in cycles of boom and burst today. There was no temple ritual that could stop it then and there is no amount of "sowing" that can stop it today. We learn how to trust in God during the different cycles without abandoning common sense and spiritual smartness.

God had given Pharaoh a word of wisdom through the imagery of dreams. Pharaoh could not relate to it as a word of wisdom until he gained understanding through the interpretation of the dream. God had given Pharaoh a 14-year economic forecast.

This dream is also significant because it is the first dream in the bible that shows that a correctly interpreted dream still requires equally correct application. Furthermore, the application is not necessarily within the dream.

Joseph did not despise dreams. He also did not go out looking for them. He was not paralysed without them. Dreams are not our primal means of communion with God. After interpreting Pharaoh's dream, Joseph does not wait for nightfall in order that he might dream how to apply the interpretation of the dream. He trusted in God who gave both the dream and its interpretation in the first instance. His trust was not in dreams. He leaned on the wisdom of God to give him the strategy on how to apply the interpretation. We know what to do by God.

Dreams in the Old Testament

For whatsoever things were written aforetime were written for our learning,
that we through patience and comfort of the scriptures might have hope.
Romans 15:4

It is fashionable today to approach the dreams of believers as though man is purely psychological. Much of what is touted as psychology does not line up with the Word. Since the bible has a lot to say about dreams, we do not have to resort to psychology as the only recourse. Since God has chosen to reveal some of His Word through dreams, we will attempt to examine all the dreams of the Old Testament.

We know that sleeping is not a consequence of the fall since God caused Adam to sleep before the fall (see Gen. 2:21). We do not know for certain if Adam or Eve dreamt before or after the fall.

What we do know is that in the bible, there is no record of any man or woman dreaming until after Noah's flood. God communicated with all these people without a single reference to dreams. This must mean that dreams have never been God's primal way of getting through to people.

The bible contains no record of any human dreaming until the days of Abraham. This does not mean that there were no dreamers prior to Abraham's day.

Abraham is the first man whose dream was recorded in the bible. Abraham's experience could also be classified as a vision but Abimelech's was the first that was definitely called a dream. The dreams of the Old Testament give us abundant proof that God can give dreams to people who are not born again. As with Cornelius' vision (see Acts 10), if God gives dreams to a sinner today, the emphasis would be on salvation or the furtherance of God's plan on the earth. It would be a means of conveying the gospel or bringing them closer to the gospel.

Abraham

And when the sun was going down, a deep sleep fell upon Abram; and, lo, an horror of great darkness fell upon him. And he said unto Abram, Know of a surety that thy seed shall be a stranger in a land that is not theirs, and shall serve them; and they shall afflict them four hundred years; And also that nation, whom they shall serve, will I judge: and afterward shall they come out with great substance. And thou shalt go to thy fathers in peace; thou shalt be buried in a good old age. But in the fourth generation they shall come hither again: for the iniquity of the Amorites is not yet full. And it came to pass, that, when the sun went down, and it was dark, behold a smoking furnace, and a burning lamp that passed between those pieces. In the same day the LORD made a covenant with

Abram, saying, Unto thy seed have I given this land, from the river of
Egypt unto the great river, the river Euphrates:
Genesis 15:12-18

All this happened while Abraham was in deep sleep. God is bound by His own Word even if He had spoken it to us in a dream.

I want you to notice that Abraham is dreaming about himself and his children. He was not dreaming about some other person's affairs or another man's family.

Genesis 15 starts with God speaking to Abraham in a vision. In that vision, God had given him an instruction that Abraham had acted upon. Abraham's obedience in acting upon God's instructions unleashed an avalanche of spiritual power that caused Abraham to go into deep sleep. It appears that Abraham had the dream immediately after the vision otherwise, Abraham had a dream while in a vision! Thus when we act upon the inward witness, we release tremendous spiritual power that flows over into our dream life.

Once the deep sleep fell upon Abraham, a whole load of spiritual transactions took place. It would appear that critical components of the Abrahamic covenant were transacted in Abraham's dream! This did not make it a less valid covenant. God spoke to Abraham while Abraham was in deep sleep and from God's perspective it was not less binding. Whether asleep or awake, Abraham is the same being to God. It was within this dream that God gave Abraham a word of wisdom spanning more than 400 years of time. In that dream, Abraham saw God represent Himself as a smoking oven and a burning torch. God was the only one who passed through the animals. Adam was watching. God had not required Abraham to walk through the animals. God had cut the covenant without requiring Abraham to fulfill any part or bargain the terms with God. It was the grace of God in action.

This episode shows that sometimes a dream is a window through which we contact and interact with the spirit realm.

Abimelech

But God came to Abimelech in a dream by night, and said to him, Behold, thou art but a dead man, for the woman which thou hast taken; for she is a man's wife. But Abimelech had not come near her: and he said, LORD, wilt thou slay also a righteous nation? Said he not unto me, She is my sister? and she, even she herself said, He is my brother: in the integrity of my heart and innocency of my hands have I done this. And God said unto him in a dream, Yea, I know that thou didst this in the integrity of thy heart; for I also withheld thee from sinning against me: therefore suffered I thee not to touch her. Now therefore restore the man his wife; for he is a prophet, and he shall pray for thee, and thou shalt live: and if thou restore her not, know thou that thou shalt surely die, thou, and all that are thine.
Genesis 20:3-7

There is no record in the bible that Abimelech had a covenant with God. As far as we can tell he was a heathen king. Yet, it was to unsaved king Abimelech that God gave one of the first dreams recorded in the bible. In that dream, Abimelech knew he was having a supernatural encounter.

In this dream, Abimelech is dreaming about himself and his family.

Abimelech had acted in good conscience towards Abraham who had told him a partial truth while hiding the fact that he and Sarah were husband and wife and not just half siblings. Thus Abimelech's dream proves that one does not need to be a saint in order to receive a God-given dream.

God delivered Abimelech from bringing premature death upon himself by committing adultery with Sarah. Abimelech was about to reap death as a result of the laws of sowing and reaping. God would not have been responsible for Abimelech's death.

Abimelech did not see his own death. He was given a word of wisdom about it. In dreams, physical death does not show up as death. If it is seen, it is conveyed in a symbolic manner.

Within that dream, God answered the prayer that Abimelech prayed in the dream. God answered it by telling Abimelech what to do once he woke from sleep.

God does not show us things through dreams about our personal life and then stop us from bringing about necessary change. The fact that He shows these things means that we can avert them! Acting on his limited righteousness, Abraham prayed for Abimelech and premature death was voided. If we know how to listen to God's voice and pray exercising our authority in Christ, there is much that looks inevitable that can be reversed through prayer for others.

God wanted to heal the relationship between Abimelech and Abraham. He told Abimelech to return Abraham's wife while Abraham prayed for Abimelech. This episode is an interesting commentary on how God protects the righteousness of His own. God does not discuss Abraham's wrong with Abimelech!

Job

Then thou scarest me with dreams, and terrifiest me through visions.
Job 7:14

During the time of Job's troubles, he had terrible dreams that terrorized him. Job assumed that these dreams and visions were from God. We do not know what he saw in detail but we know the effect on him. God-given dreams do not terrify saints. All the people that were terrified or scared of their dreams in the bible were not saints. This would indicate that Job's dream is not from God.

It is possible that Job's partial knowledge of God's true nature was projected into his dream life and caused him to respond in fear to a God-given dream. In which case, the fear was man made.

Jacob

Jacob's famous dream in which he sees angels ascending and descending a ladder placed between earth and heaven is a dream about himself. (Genesis 28:12).

> *And it came to pass at the time that the cattle conceived, that I lifted up mine eyes, and saw in a dream, and, behold, the rams which leaped upon the cattle were ringstraked, speckled, and grisled. And the angel of God spake unto me in a dream, saying, Jacob: And I said, Here am I. And he said, Lift up now thine eyes, and see, all the rams which leap upon the cattle are ringstraked, speckled, and grisled: for I have seen all that Laban doeth unto thee. I am the God of Bethel, where thou anointedst the pillar, and where thou vowedst a vow unto me: now arise, get thee out from this land, and return unto the land of thy kindred.*
> *Genesis 31:10-13*

At the time the cattle conceived, God gave Jacob a dream that showed him how to affect the genetics of the cattle. Through this means, God was providing for Jacob so Jacob could provide for his family. Jacob worked for Laban who had structured the working agreement so as to keep Jacob poor.

It was also through a dream that God reminded Jacob about the Abrahamic covenant. Through His angel in that dream, God spoke significant things to Jacob.

Jacob was warned in a dream that his uncle Laban was not going to be fair with him in his dealings. God knew that the idolatry would affect Jacob's family adversely; thus, He guided Jacob to relocate to Canaan, once again after a long time away.

We observe that in this dream, Jacob is dreaming about himself.

God then warned Laban in another dream to leave Jacob alone. Laban was not to bless Jacob or curse him. He was just to let Jacob go or face the consequences of standing in his path (see Gen 31:29).

Though God spoke to Laban in a dream, it was limited to Laban's dealings with Jacob.

And Israel took his journey with all that he had, and came to Beersheba, and offered sacrifices unto the God of his father Isaac. And God spake unto Israel in the visions of the night, and said, Jacob, Jacob. And he said, Here am I. And he said, I am God, the God of thy father: fear not to go down into Egypt; for I will there make of thee a great nation: I will go down with thee into Egypt; and I will also surely bring thee up again: and Joseph shall put his hand upon thine eyes.
Genesis 46:1-4

Jacob dialogued with God in a vision of the night. He dreamt of migrating to Egypt and becoming a great nation.

As is the norm, Jacob is dreaming about himself. It is the exception when your dream is about others.

The giving of the Law

When God first gave Israel the Law, He spoke it. His real intent was that each person know God's voice just as Abraham had known God's voice. The people thought that they would die if God spoke to them. They said unto Moses, Speak thou with us, and we will hear: but let not God speak with us, lest we die. (see Exodus 20:19).

When people prefer rules and regulations to intimacy, they fall from grace.

The Law was given to Israel before they reached Sinai (Ex 16).

When God gave Israel the Law, He spoke it out to the whole assembly at once (Exodus 20, Deut. 5).

There are two renditions of what God actually commanded Israel to do. In the first rendition, He commanded them to "watch the Sabbath"; while in the second, He commanded them to commemorate it.

To watch the Law means to recognise the "don'ts", which refers to the things to be done so as not to violate the Sabbath. Commemorating the Law means to recognise the "dos", which refers to the things that they needed to continue to do in observing the Sabbath.

Since He did not give them the Law twice, this is a tricky one.

One way of resolving this is to consider that God individually appeared to each member of that congregation in their dream and commanded those who were violating the Sabbath to watch it. He then told those who were not defiling the Sabbath to commemorate it. Each heard the Law in a way that applied to that person. That was supernatural and spectacular!

God did not only speak to the group, He spoke to the individual. When each person woke up in the morning, they told each other about the supernatural encounter that took place in each of their dreams individually. This is likely why each Jew accepted the Law when Moses gave it officially. Moses was confirming what each already knew through a dream. It demonstrates that Prophets are to confirm.

Balaam

There are some that believe that since dreams were a well-known vehicle for communicating with Prophets in the Old Testament (see Numbers 12:6), it is highly likely that Balaam's encounter involving the talking donkey and the angel actually happened in a dream.

If this is true, Balaam's dream-encounter does not take away from the gravity of the occasion. We recall that God's encounter with Abimelech and Solomon were in dreams and in those instances that did not reduce the force of the spiritual experience.

Gideon

And it came to pass the same night, that the LORD said unto him,

*Arise, get thee down unto the host; for I have delivered it into thine hand.
But if thou fear to go down, go thou with Phurah thy servant down to the
host: And thou shalt hear what they say; and afterward shall thine hands
be strengthened to go down unto the host. Then went he down with Phurah
his servant unto the outside of the armed men that were in the host. And
the Midianites and the Amalekites and all the children of the east lay
along in the valley like grasshoppers for multitude; and their camels were
without number, as the sand by the sea side for multitude. And when
Gideon was come, behold, there was a man that told a dream unto his
fellow, and said, Behold, I dreamed a dream, and, lo, a cake of barley
bread tumbled into the host of Midian, and came unto a tent, and smote
it that it fell, and overturned it, that the tent lay along. And his fellow
answered and said, This is nothing else save the sword of Gideon the son
of Joash, a man of Israel: for into his hand hath God delivered Midian,
and all the host. And it was so, when Gideon heard the telling of the
dream, and the interpretation thereof, that he worshipped, and returned
into the host of Israel, and said, Arise; for the LORD hath delivered into
your hand the host of Midian.
Judges 7:9-15*

God had given the Midianite camp into Gideon's hands, through
His Word to Gideon. God knew that Gideon was not as stirred
up as he should have been by God's Word to him.

In mercy, God told Gideon to go near the Midianite camp to go
hear them say things that would stir Gideon's hope.

Gideon arrived in time to hear two heathen men have a
conversation about a God-given dream which one of them had.
Then he heard the other soldier interpret.

This is a case of one heathen interpreting the God-given dream
of another heathen. This is a first.

From Gideon's perspective that interpretation was accurate!

The interpretation caused both soldiers as well as their armies to concede defeat to Gideon.

Gideon then trusted God to know how to apply the interpretation. The dreamer had dreamt, the interpreter had interpreted, and now its application was up to Gideon. Though all heard the same dream and interpretation, all were not going to apply it the same way. Gideon received it as a wake-up call for his army to seize the initiative in battle.

The bible does not say that Gideon's army had any weapons. They just had trumpets, pitchers and lamps (see Judges 7:16).

Gideon instructed his soldiers to shout, "The sword of the Lord, and of Gideon".

This was the exact phrase that had been used in the interpretation of the dream. Somehow, when the Midianites heard that sound, they would have taken it as supernatural validation of the interpretation given to the soldier's dream. This planted into the heart of soldiers in that vast army the image of hopelessness and utter defeat, which caused them to fight each other. Defeat had been imparted to them through the interpretation of a dream.

Once again, the person dreaming was dreaming about himself or herself. This dream was used to supply defeat to the person dreaming and to all those that believed his interpretation. Either the dreamer, the interpreter or both were people whose words carried a lot of weight with people.

It is not what others see that causes you to fail or succeed. It is what you believe based on what they have seen or spoken that matters.

This is a spiritually significant dream that shows how people's hearts can cause them to fail through the images fed into their hearts by spoken words. The same dream that was used to minister discouragement to the enemy was used to minister encouragement to Gideon. All heard the same interpretation. The difference was how they applied it. Application is the last phase of the dream cycle. First the dream, then the interpretation and lastly its application.

Solomon

In Gibeon the LORD appeared to Solomon in a dream by night: and God said, Ask what I shall give thee. And Solomon said, Thou hast shewed unto thy servant David my father great mercy, according as he walked before thee in truth, and in righteousness, and in uprightness of heart with thee; and thou hast kept for him this great kindness, that thou hast given him a son to sit on his throne, as it is this day. And now, O LORD my God, thou hast made thy servant king instead of David my father: and I am but a little child: I know not how to go out or come in. And thy servant is in the midst of thy people which thou hast chosen, a great people, that cannot be numbered nor counted for multitude. Give therefore thy servant an understanding heart to judge thy people, that I may discern between good and bad: for who is able to judge this thy so great a people? And the speech pleased the LORD, that Solomon had asked this thing. And God said unto him, Because thou hast asked this thing, and hast not asked for thyself long life; neither hast asked riches for thyself, nor hast asked the life of thine enemies; but hast asked for thyself understanding to discern judgment; Behold, I have done according to thy words: lo, I have given thee a wise and an understanding heart; so that there was none like thee before thee, neither after thee shall any arise like unto thee. And I have also given thee that which thou hast not asked, both riches, and honour: so that there shall not be any among the kings like unto thee all thy days. And if thou wilt walk in my ways, to keep

*my statutes and my commandments, as thy father David did walk, then I
will lengthen thy days. And Solomon awoke; and, behold, it was a dream.
And he came to Jerusalem, and stood before the ark of the covenant of
the LORD, and offered up burnt offerings, and offered peace offerings, and
made a feast to all his servants.*
1 Kings 3:5-15

Some dreams are encounters with the spirit realm. This is one of
them. Solomon prayed to God in his dream and God answered
it within that dream. God was pleased with the request that
Solomon made in his request within his dream!

Solomon is famed for his unusual measure of wisdom. This
wisdom was not the product of his father's blessing or a result
of his attending some convention where a prophet laid hands
upon him. It was something intensely personal between him and
the Lord. It was an intense impartation of wisdom through a
dream. Solomon's dream was a window through which he was
interacting with the spirit realm. His dream was spiritual reality.

In this dream, the Lord appeared to him and imparted wisdom
into Solomon in an unusual degree. It was beyond a measure
that any other Old Testament figure had been exposed to. The
fact that this took place in a dream did not make it less real.
Solomon woke up from sleep and the impartation of wisdom
overflowed from the spirit realm into his life.

We notice that in this dream, Solomon was dreaming about
himself.

Daniel

*As for these four children, God gave them knowledge and skill in all
learning and wisdom: and Daniel had understanding in all visions and*

dreams.
Daniel 1:17

We observe that Daniel had understanding in all visions and dreams. This was not natural or as a result of someone laying hands on him. It was a supernatural faculty deposited into him by the Spirit of God.

Daniel exercised this ability as he depended upon God and waited upon Him. He expected God to reveal the meaning of dreams to him. When he was under the anointing he could unravel any vision or dream, even if those visions and dreams were other people's experiences. He was so developed in this gift that he could recollect a dream that another person had dreamt and then proceed to tell its interpretation.

Daniel did not begin a dream interpretation ministry as a result of this. Daniel did not interpret the dream of Shedrach, Meshach or Abednego. He interpreted the dreams of the heathen kings. His interpretations caused the kings to admit the greatness of God at work in Daniel.

As a result of his prophetic office, Daniel was twice given revelations about the kingdoms that would come in the future (see Daniel 7 & 8). Thus Daniel's dreams about the four beasts as well as the one about the ram and the goat were dreams about others.

Nebuchadnezzar

And the king said unto them, I have dreamed a dream, and my spirit was troubled to know the dream. Then spake the Chaldeans to the king in Syriack, O king, live for ever: tell thy servants the dream, and we will shew the interpretation. The king answered and said to the Chaldeans,

The thing is gone from me: if ye will not make known unto me the dream, with the interpretation thereof, ye shall be cut in pieces, and your houses shall be made a dunghill. But if ye shew the dream, and the interpretation thereof, ye shall receive of me gifts and rewards and great honour: therefore shew me the dream, and the interpretation thereof. Then Daniel went in, and desired of the king that he would give him time, and that he would shew the king the interpretation. Then Daniel went to his house, and made the thing known to Hananiah, Mishael, and Azariah, his companions: That they would desire mercies of the God of heaven concerning this secret; that Daniel and his fellows should not perish with the rest of the wise men of Babylon. Then was the secret revealed unto Daniel in a night vision. Then Daniel blessed the God of heaven. Daniel answered and said, Blessed be the name of God for ever and ever: for wisdom and might are his: And he changeth the times and the seasons: he removeth kings, and setteth up kings: he giveth wisdom unto the wise, and knowledge to them that know understanding: He revealeth the deep and secret things: he knoweth what is in the darkness, and the light dwelleth with him. I thank thee, and praise thee, O thou God of my fathers, who hast given me wisdom and might, and hast made known unto me now what we desired of thee: for thou hast now made known unto us the king's matter. But there is a God in heaven that revealeth secrets, and maketh known to the king Nebuchadnezzar what shall be in the latter days. Thy dream, and the visions of thy head upon thy bed, are these; As for thee, O king, thy thoughts came into thy mind upon thy bed, what should come to pass hereafter: and he that revealeth secrets maketh known to thee what shall come to pass. But as for me, this secret is not revealed to me for any wisdom that I have more than any living, but for their sakes that shall make known the interpretation to the king, and that thou mightest know the thoughts of thy heart.
Daniel 2:3-6, 16-23, 28-30

Nebuchadnezzar took the matter of dreaming to a whole new level. He wanted someone to interpret his dream to him, though he had not told him or her the details of the dream beforehand.

What was Nebuchadnezzar's immediate response to the dream?

He was afraid.

Nebuchadnezzar was so frightened of the imagery within his dream that he forgot it. Fear drains our memory of its power.

We observe that Daniel was not a performer but a minister of God. He knew not to make haste. He asked for time. The flesh hurries. Faith exercises patience.

He obtained interpretation through prayer. Daniel's prayer released so much tremendous power that it produced visions in him that night. Daniel saw in a vision of the night, what Nebuchadnezzar had seen in a dream.

Through this dream, God had given Nebuchadnezzar a revelation about the kingdoms that would come after his.

The kingdom of God is symbolised by the stone that Nebuchadnezzar saw in this dream.

> *This is the dream; and we will tell the interpretation thereof before the king. Thou, O king, art a king of kings: for the God of heaven hath given thee a kingdom, power, and strength, and glory. And wheresoever the children of men dwell, the beasts of the field and the fowls of the heaven hath he given into thine hand, and hath made thee ruler over them all.*
> *Thou art this head of gold.*
> *Daniel 2:36-38*

Notice that Daniel had accurately pointed out to Nebuchadnezzar, "You are the head of gold."

Now it is one thing to get correct interpretation but correct interpretation is not all there is to a dream. After we get the interpretation, we must get the correct application. Following on from Daniel's interpretation, in a bizarre twist Nebuchadnezzar spectacularly applied the dream wrongly. His pride coloured everything. He should have humbled himself as a result of that dream; since he had been informed about the stone that was capable of levelling his kingdom and all that will come after his. Nebuchadnezzar did not like that; so his pride cherry-picked what caught his fancy. He conveniently forgot that the dream was really about that stone.

After hearing the interpretation, Nebuchadnezzar should also have prayed until he really grasped the intent of Danie's excellent interpretation. Pride messed up a powerful God-given dream. No, the dream was not the problem, the dreamer was not developed enough to use it well. Whether you dream or not, be a person of the Word and give yourself to prayer.

He had to be the centre of everything.

His pride kept echoing, "You are the head of gold."

He tried to take guidance from a dream. He should have approached God through His Word. He should have prayed. He should have discussed further with Daniel to understand the interpretation. He assumed.

We must realise that a dream does not confer spirituality, maturity or spiritual growth. Nebuchadnezzar's heathen mind-set caused him to use Daniel's words as a foundation for his desire for self-worship, which resulted in idolatry. He built a statue that all were to worship. He started a religion on the back of a God-given dream! This still happens today.

Nebuchadnezzar was not dreaming about himself. He was dreaming about others.

Nebuchadnezzar had another dream.

*I Nebuchadnezzar was at rest in mine house, and flourishing in my palace:
I saw a dream which made me afraid, and the thoughts upon my bed and
the visions of my head troubled me. Therefore made I a decree to bring
in all the wise men of Babylon before me, that they might make known
unto me the interpretation of the dream. Then came in the magicians, the
astrologers, the Chaldeans, and the soothsayers: and I told the dream before
them; but they did not make known unto me the interpretation thereof.
But at the last Daniel came in before me, whose name was Belteshazzar,
according to the name of my God, and in whom is the spirit of the holy
gods: and before him I told the dream, saying, O Belteshazzar, master of
the magicians, because I know that the spirit of the holy gods is in thee,
and no secret troubleth thee, tell me the visions of my dream that I have
seen, and the interpretation thereof. Thus were the visions of mine head in
my bed; I saw, and behold a tree in the midst of the earth, and the height
thereof was great. The tree grew, and was strong, and the height thereof
reached unto heaven, and the sight thereof to the end of all the earth: The
leaves thereof were fair, and the fruit thereof much, and in it was meat
for all: the beasts of the field had shadow under it, and the fowls of the
heaven dwelt in the boughs thereof, and all flesh was fed of it. I saw in the
visions of my head upon my bed, and, behold, a watcher and an holy one
came down from heaven; He cried aloud, and said thus, Hew down the
tree, and cut off his branches, shake off his leaves, and scatter his fruit:
let the beasts get away from under it, and the fowls from his branches:
Nevertheless leave the stump of his roots in the earth, even with a band
of iron and brass, in the tender grass of the field; and let it be wet with
the dew of heaven, and let his portion be with the beasts in the grass of
the earth: Let his heart be changed from man's, and let a beast's heart
be given unto him; and let seven times pass over him. This matter is by
the decree of the watchers, and the demand by the word of the holy ones:
to the intent that the living may know that the most High ruleth in the
kingdom of men, and giveth it to whomsoever he will, and setteth up over
it the basest of men. This dream I king Nebuchadnezzar have seen. Now*

thou, O Belteshazzar, declare the interpretation thereof, forasmuch as all the wise men of my kingdom are not able to make known unto me the interpretation: but thou art able; for the spirit of the holy gods is in thee. Then Daniel, whose name was Belteshazzar, was astonied for one hour, and his thoughts troubled him. The king spake, and said, Belteshazzar, let not the dream, or the interpretation thereof, trouble thee. Belteshazzar answered and said, My lord, the dream be to them that hate thee, and the interpretation thereof to thine enemies. The tree that thou sawest, which grew, and was strong, whose height reached unto the heaven, and the sight thereof to all the earth; Whose leaves were fair, and the fruit thereof much, and in it was meat for all; under which the beasts of the field dwelt, and upon whose branches the fowls of the heaven had their habitation: It is thou, O king, that art grown and become strong: for thy greatness is grown, and reacheth unto heaven, and thy dominion to the end of the earth.

Daniel 4:4-22

Through this dream, God had warned Nebuchadnezzar about the psychological consequences of pride. God was telling Nebuchadnezzar that his famous wilderness experience where he would function like a wild beast was not destined. That experience was avoidable. There is much that is labelled destiny that is nothing more than not being smart enough to make adjustments that would bring about different outcomes in life.

In a bizarre twist, Nebuchadnezzar listened to Daniel's excellent interpretation but chose to remain in pride! Nebuchadnezzar reaped insanity from his pride.

His pride brought about his fall and he harvested needless psychological tragedy by sowing to his flesh. The experience of Nebuchadnezzar was man-made. It did not reflect God's anger. It reflected man's rejection of God's mercy.

We observe that in this dream, Nebuchadnezzar was dreaming

about himself although he did not appear in his own dream as himself. He appeared as a tree. He had twelve months within which to repent but he would not.

The tree that thou sawest, which grew, and was strong, whose height reached unto the heaven, and the sight thereof to all the earth; Whose leaves were fair, and the fruit thereof much, and in it was meat for all; under which the beasts of the field dwelt, and upon whose branches the fowls of the heaven had their habitation: It is thou, O king, that art grown and become strong: for thy greatness is grown, and reacheth unto heaven, and thy dominion to the end of the earth. And whereas the king saw a watcher and an holy one coming down from heaven, and saying, Hew the tree down, and destroy it; yet leave the stump of the roots thereof in the earth, even with a band of iron and brass, in the tender grass of the field; and let it be wet with the dew of heaven, and let his portion be with the beasts of the field, till seven times pass over him; This is the interpretation, O king, and this is the decree of the most High, which is come upon my lord the king: That they shall drive thee from men, and thy dwelling shall be with the beasts of the field, and they shall make thee to eat grass as oxen, and they shall wet thee with the dew of heaven, and seven times shall pass over thee, till thou know that the most High ruleth in the kingdom of men, and giveth it to whomsoever he will. And whereas they commanded to leave the stump of the tree roots; thy kingdom shall be sure unto thee, after that thou shalt have known that the heavens do rule. Wherefore, O king, let my counsel be acceptable unto thee, and break off thy sins by righteousness, and thine iniquities by shewing mercy to the poor; if it may be a lengthening of thy tranquillity.
Daniel 4:20-27

Nebuchadnezzar's dream occurred in two phases. The first phase conveyed the fact that Nebuchadnezzar was growing in influence and prosperity. His kingdom was getting established.

The second phase contained some divine warnings about adjustments that Nebuchadnezzar needed to make, in order to correct his prideful heart and avoid judgment.

This shows that a dream does not have to have a single message.

We notice from this dream that our dreams do not generally deal with the distant future. Our dreams can talk about the distant future as was the case with Joseph but that is not the norm. They deal with the present and things we need to do in the immediate.

This dream showed the positive aspects of Nebuchadnezzar's life and then also focused on the aspects where Nebuchadnezzar needed to repent.

Daniel did not dream this about Nebuchadnezzar; it was Nebuchadnezzar who dreamt this about himself.

As a general principle, your dreams would be about yourself, even if you see other people in the dream. Your dreams are not telling you something about them. They tell you about yourself. This is the case because there are things about ourselves we are unwilling to see directly. The message gets passed using our perceptions of others to tell us something about ourselves.

Interpreting the dream of others

Interpreting the dream of others is not a ministry from one saint to another. It is the heathen that interpreted each other's dreams (Judges 7:13-14).

In fact, throughout God's Word, Joseph and Daniel are the only saints who interpreted the dreams of the heathen. They were the exception and not the norm. God gave both men the ability to interpret the dream of others, in order to give them exalted office and influence in the kingdom of heathen kings so as to bring about the plan of God on the earth.

Moving into the present

If all that you see in your dreams is that which relates to something, which occurred in your distant past, it might indicate that there are unresolved things for you to sort out. Our dreams should catch up to reflect present day aspects of our lives.

As a teenager, Joseph saw himself binding sheaf.

Pharaoh saw himself **as a man** standing by the Nile.

The Baker and the Butler each saw themselves as Baker and Butler respectively.

None of these individuals were stuck in their past. They were all dreaming about things that reflected their present station in life as at the time of their dream.

These individuals were developing and advancing in life. Dreams can be helpful in this regard. If the recurring theme of your dreams is in the past, it might be symptomatic of things that you need to get sorted by God's Word in order for you to progress onto the next phase of your life.

Don't get caught up with dreams

For in the multitude of dreams and many words there are also divers vanities: but fear thou God.
Ecclesiastes 5:7

Dreaming many dreams does not make the dreamer spiritual. In fact, Solomon warns against getting caught up with a multitude of dreams. One can be engrossed in dreams and yet not understand the fear of God.

Application, Interpretation and Revelation

Thus far in the Old Testament we notice that there are three parts to dreams – application, interpretation and revelation. The revelation or disclosure aspect is the first stage, which is the dream itself. There is hardly any problem in that arena. The challenge is in the interpretation stage where people attempt fleshly interpretations which breed confusion. Most times, we are unaware of the importance of the application stage, which is the last stage. Too many times. the progression from revelation to interpretation causes much shipwreck. If the interpretation is wrong, the application cannot be right.

Dreams of historic significance

We also notice that the Old Testament dreams that were global, notable and of historic importance were usually dreamt by Kings, a member of the king's cabinet or Prophets and not by the ordinary people.

These dreams tended to cover a longer time frame of fulfilment. Thus, people dream in line with the extent of their authority. Therefore, you would not dream about people that you have no relationship with or are unable to influence. If you do, the people are symbolic. They represent something about you or your attitude towards them.

The dreams of those who were neither prophets nor kings were personal in scope and dealt with the immediate needs of the dreamer. They also sometimes dealt with the family of the dreamer. This is consistent with the fact that you dream in line with the extent of your authority. You wouldn't ordinarily dream about another man's family. If you do, you are seeing how that affects you or lessons you should learn from it. It is about you and not about them.

Since God is not a talebearer, if He chooses to show you something about another person through a dream, His intention is not to embarrass that person but to protect you as you relate to the person. The emphasis is still not that person but you; except of course, He is showing you because the person falls within your sphere of influence, or so you can pray for that person.

All God-given dreams are given to further God's will.

Joseph and his brethren interpreted a dream whose fulfilment was about 13 years away when Joseph would be a ruler in Egypt. Joseph himself later interpreted Pharaoh's dream, which was at least fourteen years in the future. Daniel interpreted Nebuchadnezzar's dream whose time frame was centuries in the future. Then Daniel had a dream that was way out. I believe that Daniel struggled to interpret this because he had seen things that were too far ahead of his generation. He had seen thousands of years into the future. Human civilisation would have changed and he did not have the language, experience or culture against which to draw upon in order to put these things into words.

The bible records only a few dreams and many of those dreams occurred together as a cluster in certain books with no dreams recorded in the overwhelming majority of the books of the Old Testament. In total, there are sixteen definite God-given dreams recorded in the Old Testament. Of these, three are in the book of Daniel, and one each in Kings and Judges. In the book of Genesis alone, we have eleven dreams. This makes Genesis a book about dreams as much as anything else.

Dreams in the New Testament

It is worthy of note that Matthew is the only writer in the New Testament portion of the bible who gives actual dream records. The record of New Testament life, which is God's life in man after the ascension of Jesus, is significantly silent on dreams. From the book of Acts onwards, which coincides with the coming of the Spirit at Pentecost onwards, we find a drastic reduction in the record of dreams. We find an increase in visions. This is because visions do not require you to be asleep while dreams do. The implication is that through the New Birth, we can be conscious of God getting through to us at any time.

Joseph

The New Covenant was not in effect when Joseph had all his dreams. There could be no New Covenant until Jesus rose from the dead and presented His blood in Heaven. For this reason, Joseph's dreams are Old Testament dreams.

But while he thought on these things, behold, the angel of the LORD appeared unto him in a dream, saying, Joseph, thou son of David, fear not to take unto thee Mary thy wife: for that which is conceived in her is of the Holy Ghost. And she shall bring forth a son, and thou shalt call his name JESUS: for he shall save his people from their sins. Now all this was done, that it might be fulfilled which was spoken of the Lord by the prophet, saying, Behold, a virgin shall be with child, and shall bring forth a son, and they shall call his name Emmanuel, which being interpreted is, God with us. Then Joseph being raised from sleep did as the angel of the Lord had bidden him, and took unto him his wife:
Matthew 1:20-25

While Joseph thought about how to privately put away Mary without putting her life in danger, he fell asleep. Through a dream, he received divine confirmation from the angel of the Lord that Mary truly carried a supernatural conception. This is a significant dream because it clearly shows that God will still work with His Word even in your dreams. God-given dreams help people get back to the Word. God reminded Joseph of Isaiah's prophecy. It was relatively easy for God to get through to Joseph because Joseph already knew Isaiah's prophecy.

God used His Word that was already in Joseph's life to sort out Joseph's psychological trauma. You see, God's Word is authentic psychiatric treatment. Meditate on the Word until you become Word-possessed (which is to be God-possessed since the Word is God). The Word will become your encourager, counselor and manager. Drift into sleep and let the spirit of God's Word within you cause you to hear God and dream of God; for God is in His Word.

In Joseph's dreams, we notice a fundamental principle that the dream calls the dreamer to action. If you see other people taking action in your dream, you should trust God to communicate to them the steps that they need to take. Your dream tells you what you should get done and not what they should do.

Joseph was dreaming about himself and his family.

Out of Egypt have I called my Son

Shortly after the visit of the Magi from the East, Joseph had another dream.

And when they were departed, behold, the angel of the Lord appeareth to Joseph in a dream, saying, Arise, and take the young child and his mother, and flee into Egypt, and be thou there until I bring thee word: for Herod will seek the young child to destroy him. When he arose, he took the young child and his mother by night, and departed into Egypt: And was there until the death of Herod: that it might be fulfilled which was spoken of the Lord by the prophet, saying, Out of Egypt have I called my son.
Matthew 2:13-15

Joseph's dream about where to take Jesus and Mary was a dream of guidance. He received guidance not just about the need to leave Israel but where he was to take the young family. It was by spectacular means that he knew to flee into Egypt. That statement, "out of Egypt have I called my son" is in Hosea. In Joseph's dreams, we notice that the spirit of God's Word within Joseph caused him to dream of God, for God is in His Word. Joseph became a migrant in Egypt based on God's Word.

Hosea observed that when God called Israel out of Egypt, they turned to idol worship instead of Jehovah; thus implying, they did not fulfil God's reason for calling them out of Egypt (see

Hosea 11:1-2). When Matthew says, "that it might be fulfilled", he is saying that Jesus is the son that God called out of Egypt to fulfil the mandate of redemption that Israel could not. Jesus is the correct explanation of the Exodus. Jesus is the Exodus that fulfilled God's intent. The point is that Jesus succeeded where Israel had failed. Matthew is saying that Jesus is Israel's story properly retold, for He filled up all that was lacking in the Old Testament accounts.

Again, we observe that Joseph was dreaming about himself and his family.

After the death of Herod, we find Joseph dreaming again.

But when Herod was dead, behold, an angel of the Lord appeareth in a dream to Joseph in Egypt, Saying, Arise, and take the young child and his mother, and go into the land of Israel: for they are dead which sought the young child's life. And he arose, and took the young child and his mother, and came into the land of Israel. But when he heard that Archelaus did reign in Judaea in the room of his father Herod, he was afraid to go thither: notwithstanding, being warned of God in a dream, he turned aside into the parts of Galilee:
Matthew 2:22-23

This contains two dreams. In the first, while in Egypt, an Angel gave Joseph a word of knowledge that Herod had died and that it was safe to return to Israel. The second dream only came about after Joseph had acted on the first dream. We do not know if he saw an Angel in the second dream. The second dream came when he was in the borders of Israel. Through that second dream, he received guidance not to return to the land from which he came. He was divinely guided to settle in Nazareth. In that sense, both dreams were related and the second was a continuation of the first. The second was more specific than the first.

Once more, we note that Joseph was dreaming about himself and his family.

The Wise Men

And when they were come into the house, they saw the young child with Mary his mother, and fell down, and worshipped him: and when they had opened their treasures, they presented unto him gifts; gold, and frankincense and myrrh. And being warned of God in a dream that they should not return to Herod, they departed into their own country another way.
Matthew 2:12

There is no bible evidence that the Magi were three men. They were definitely wise. Wise men still seek Jesus. There is also no evidence that they ever met Jesus in a manger. They met him in a house and not in a manger. They also did not meet Jesus as a baby but as a little boy.

More importantly, the Magi had a God-given dream after they had seen Jesus and were on their way back to Herod. Through that dream, they received warning not to return to Herod. This was a dream of guidance.

Since they were warned of God in a dream, it is likely that each of them was given the same dream. This is how they would have received boldness that the right course of action was not to go to King Herod. Herod had told them that he also wanted to worship the new-born king. He was being deceitful and the wise men did not know any better, for Herod hid his murderous intentions from the wise men. God saw through it all and therefore instructed the wise men not return to Herod.

Once again, we observe that the Magi dreamt about what they were to do. They did not dream about what Herod should do.

Pilate's Wife

When he was set down on the judgment seat, his wife sent unto him,
saying, Have thou nothing to do with that just man: for I have suffered
many things this day in a dream because of him.
Matthew 27:19

One of the most intriguing dreams mentioned in the bible is that
of Pilate's wife around the time Pilate was judging Jesus' case.
Pilate's wife appears and vanishes in a single verse. Her testimony
is important for she testified of the innocence of Jesus.

We do not know whether Pilate dreamt. This dream was not one
that Pilate's wife could shake off easily. It was so significant that
she sent an urgent message to halt proceedings and arrest the
attention of her husband, who sat on the throne of judgment.
Pilate was the one with the legal power to execute Jesus. The
Jews didn't have that power.

Pilate's wife did not have this dream at night. She said, "I have
suffered many things this day in a dream". It is implied that all
bible dreams are night dreams. Pilate's wife's dream is therefore
unusual.

Jesus had to die on the cross on a specific day, the Passover day.
He could not die any other way and at any other time and still
fulfil scripture.

Jesus was to die by God's determinate counsel and foreknowledge
of God. He was also to die by wicked hands. Pilate was given
evidence through his wife's witness confirming that Jesus was
a just man. Pilate ignored his wife's witness. It was not a sin of
ignorance. This confirms that he was a wicked man.

Pilate's wife was convinced of Jesus' innocence through a dream.

She instructed her husband not to have anything to do with that case, as a result of her dream.

Notice that her dream called her or her husband to action. Her dream did not tell Jesus or the High Priest what to do. In this case, Pilate did not necessarily heed her counsel.

Is every dream God-given?

It is a peculiar fact that the bible does not record dreams that are not good. This we must admit. In fact, all the dreams whose details are recorded in the bible have a positive slant to them. In the light of this, many assume that every dream is from God.

Is this so?

While the bible does not give us the record of a false dream, there are numerous references within the bible letting us in on the fact that there are false dreams. Some of these dreams may even appear "prophetic" at first.

Which think to cause my people to forget my name by their dreams which they tell every man to his neighbour, as their fathers have forgotten my name for Baal. Behold, I am against them that prophesy false dreams, saith the LORD, and do tell them, and cause my people to err by their lies, and by their lightness; yet I sent them not, nor commanded them: therefore they shall not profit this people at all, saith the LORD.
Jeremiah 23:27, 32

For thus saith the LORD of hosts, the God of Israel; Let not your prophets and your diviners, that be in the midst of you, deceive you, neither hearken to your dreams which ye cause to be dreamed. For they prophesy falsely unto you in my name: I have not sent them, saith the LORD.
Jeremiah 29:8-9

Prophets can have prophetic dreams that are lies. Prophetic dreams are not necessarily true just because a nationally syndicated prophet dreamt them. We still have a more sure Word than the revelations contained within a prophet's dream. You do not consider the stature, office or standing of the person that had the dream, you consider the Lord and what He has said in His Word. You judge everything in the light of what Christ has accomplished in redemption.

The bible does not tell us that all dreams are good. There are false dreams just as there are good ones. A good dream emphasises the voice of the good shepherd to you. A false dream imparts confusion and robs you of confidence in God.

A dream is good when it stirs up the spirit of faith.

Some would point out that the bible only advices caution in relation to listening to or making decisions based on the dream of others (Deut. 13:1-5, Jer. 14:14, Jer. 23:16, 25-27, 27:9-11, Ezek. 13:1,7, 12:24).

This school of thought points out that there is no warning against personal dreams, therefore they conclude that all our personal dreams are positive.

Are we to embrace all of our personal dreams?

The Prophet Jeremiah foretold the fact that many dreams are not of God, in that they are lies (see Jeremiah 23:31-32).

A lie is that which leads people to doubt the finished work of

Christ.

If a dream injures your security in Christ or your confidence in His ability to put you over in life, it is a lie. If anyone prophesies such dreams to you, they might be genuine but they are prophesying lies in the name of the Lord.

You have a God-given responsibility not to allow such dreams or dreamers in your world. In reality, God is not the one that permits such ministries, you do. Your first job is not to listen to such in the first place (see Jeremiah 29:8-9).

We must not approach our dreams or interpret our dreams in a way that undoes the finished work of Christ or tosses away our precious redemption, as though it was an afterthought. It is the same God that is behind God-given dreams, who is also behind the marvellous redemption that we have in Christ. There is no conflict in God, therefore we should not entertain anything that belittles what Christ has accomplished. If it is the same God that commended His love towards us in His Son that gave us a dream, that dream cannot give God a voice that crucifies Jesus afresh.

God compares the spiritual effect of His Word to wheat (see Jer. 23:28-32).. Wheat is nourishing. You can feed on it. In the same vein, He compares dreams to chaff. You cannot feed on chaff. There is no stability or nourishment in chaff. Chaff is tossed to and fro by the wind. Therefore people who base their lives on dreams are like chaff before the wind. Dreams can carry a degree of revelation but the degree of revelation carried by the Word of God is of a far higher quality and substance than that carried by dreams. Dreams are to be treated as a far lower level of inspiration and revelation to the pure Word of God. Dreams are not always reliable but the Word of God is tried and true!

The Word of God will burn away silly dreams. The more you are full of God's Word, the less your life would be governed by dreams. The Word in you will smash those false dreams, which would have robbed you of your consciousness of a complete redemption in Christ. God's Word is so powerful it will burn off the folly contained within even those dreams we treat as prophetic. God's Word will open up your spiritual faculties and cause your spiritual eyesight to be sharp.

You do not become better at dreaming by listening to other people's dreams or by having some Prophet retell their dreams to you. You become better at dreaming by feasting on God's Word.

Asking God for dreams?

The New Testament epistles encourage us to pray that the eyes of our understanding be open through the spirit of wisdom and revelation of His Word. We are not instructed to desire or ask the Holy Spirit to give us dreams (see Eph. 1:16).

No one in the bible ever prayed for God to speak to him or her through a dream. Daniel prayed to God to reveal to him Nebuchadnezzar's dream and its interpretation. Even then Daniel did not ask God to give him a dream. He trusted God to pass that information on however He saw fit. Daniel had the gift of interpretation of dreams and visions, so he expected that through prayer God would operate the gift as He deemed fit.

Those that God chose to speak to through dreams were just going about their daily lives when those dreams were given. Thus we would not be scriptural, if we were to ask God to speak to us in a dream. It is up to him to choose that medium and it is our responsibility to be open to His Word and His methods. If we let the flesh pressure us into asking God to give us a dream, we would be providing satan all the incentive he needs to supply confusion into our lives. Usually, those that are eager to have these dreams are not ready for it and wouldn't know what to do with a God-given dream.

The defence that we have in God's Word and the inward witness is more than enough. If God sees fit to add to that through dreams, so be it.

What about dreams about coming disaster?

God-given dreams are to be judged in the light of the fact that God is not angry with men, and that He is not holding their sins against them. He has not changed His mind towards men. If our dreams make it look like God is holding men's sins against them, we either re-examine our dreams or reconsider our interpretation of it. God-given dreams carry the same inspiration as prophecy.

Biblical prophecy edifies, exhorts and comforts (see 1 Cor. 14:3). One of satan's chief characteristic is that he operates strongly in discouragement and condemnation. Therefore just like prophecy, God-given dreams would nullify satan's weapon of discouragement and condemnation.

Yea, when they had made them a molten calf, and said, This is thy God that brought thee up out of Egypt, and had wrought great provocations; Yet thou in thy manifold mercies forsookest them not in the wilderness: the pillar of the cloud departed not from them by day, to lead them in the way; neither the pillar of fire by night, to shew them light, and the way wherein they should go.
Nehemiah 9:18-19

Even in the Old Testament under the Law, Nehemiah had a revelation of God's mercy. As we consider the fact that God did not forsake Israel even when they provoked Him in the wilderness, we marvel at the loving-kindness of God. God's mercy is in its fullest expression in the Lord Jesus. It is because of what God has wrought in redemption through Christ that our eyes are opened at last to see how merciful God really is. The tragedies they experienced in the wilderness were because they forsook God's mercy through unbelief. God never forsook them.

But let us, who are of the day, be sober, putting on the breastplate of faith and love; and for an helmet, the hope of salvation. For God hath not appointed us to wrath, but to obtain salvation by our Lord Jesus Christ,
1 Thessalonians 5:8-9

This reveals the heart of God regarding wrath. The Lord Jesus has not gone to great lengths to deliver the people that God is looking for ways to vent frustration, venom and anger on. Instead, God's end game for the saint is not wrath but salvation through the Lord Jesus Christ.

Jesus is the basis for God's mercy, nothing else is – not even our prayers. Prayer has its place. Our prayers wear down the cooperation and power that men supply to satan through unbelief. Even when men are in unbelief, God will seek every avenue to show that His mercy prevails over judgment (James 2:13).

Some of what people call warning dreams of judgment communicates discouragement and condemnation; therefore, they are not of God. These dreams indicate impending unavoidable disaster. These dreamers dream as though Christ has not died. Their dreams promote fatalism. They mostly assume that the more apocalyptic their dream, the more likely it is that it is divine in origin. Therefore, they simply pass on these dreams into the wider Christian community without first judging it in the light of redemption.

It is true that God can send warnings about judgment through dreams. When God sends this type of warning, the mercy of God still shines through. God does not give warning dreams so as to guarantee wrath. He gives it so that wrath may be averted (Isaiah 59:16, Ezek. 22:30-31, Jer. 5:1). Nebuchadnezzar had a warning dream of impending judgment (see Dan. 4:27-34). Nebuchadnezzar had twelve months of extended mercy in which to repent, after he had dreamt of judgment. By refusing to repent, Nebuchadnezzar forsook the mercy of God.

Satan often camouflages as an angel of light seeking to give false enlightenment that invalidates what Christ has wrought in redemption. Satan delights in stealing, killing and destroying our comprehension of God's goodness (see John. 10:10). While God neither delights in nor is interested in the death of the sinner satan is! We must not fail to understand that satan is a murderer who holds our sins against us. If we do, we receive these dreams of judgment assume that just because it promises death to the sinner, then it is God who is behind it.

Wherefore, when I came, was there no man? when I called, was there none to answer? Is my hand shortened at all, that it cannot redeem? or have I no power to deliver? behold, at my rebuke I dry up the sea, I make the rivers a wilderness: their fish stinketh, because there is no water, and dieth for thirst.
Isaiah 50:2

The Lord Jesus has extended God's delivering power to man through His death, burial and resurrection. The effect of this is reaped through men, who supply this delivering power through prayer. There is no deficiency of mercy in God. Therefore, we are not setting ourselves in prayer to make Him show mercy instead of anger. If God needs to show more mercy, where would He get it anyway? We must not be like Moses begging God not to destroy the people; for that would mean we are praying because God is angry. We pray for people in this instance because people are sowing and reaping satanic destruction. Through our prayers, we are holding back the judgment that men draw upon themselves because of their blind minds. When people persist in sin, God does not hold back His mercy; instead, it is people that forsake their own mercies! (Jonah 2:8).

God definitely sends warnings.

When God sends warnings, the overriding feeling is that of hope and not of doom. The hearers perceive the protecting hand of the Lord and they understand that there is a way out. God always provides a way of escape through repentance. When the saints repent it is not so they might go to heaven, but as a means of receiving God's protection from the curse released by satan into this earth through Adam. Unbelief causes people to shun repentance. Unbelief is the sin that causes people to cooperate with satan. This banishes God's protective presence and gives place to the devil who delights in wreaking havoc and wiping out communities indiscriminately. Repentance increases the manifest footprint of God's protective presence (see Ezek. 33:11). We should not be looking for reasons why people should be destroyed but how to preserve them; in order that they might hear the Gospel and respond in faith.

Satan holds people's sins against them and he uses this to wreak havoc. A scriptural warning inspires believers to pray, so as to use their high privilege to lose the mercy that is available in Christ. At the same time, we pray so as to suspend the advantage satan has over people through ignorance and blindness. The knowledge of God's nature and what Jesus has accomplished must govern how we pray for others, especially those we are convinced that God is angry with. (see author's book, Prayernomics). Scriptural warnings stir up men to repent by agreeing with Jesus instead of abiding in unbelief.

With my soul have I desired thee in the night; yea, with my spirit within me will I seek thee early: for when thy judgments are in the earth, the inhabitants of the world will learn righteousness.
Isaiah 26:9

God sends His warnings so that the very men for whom Christ died may retrieve themselves from satan's trap and snare. God's warnings do not give satan the advantage, it empowers men to withdraw from unbelief and cooperate with the mercy of God instead.

Some of these concepts can be seen in King Abimelech's dream (see Genesis 20:1-18). God showed that the judgment was conditional. It was a warning dream of impending judgment if he committed adultery with Sarah. Since this dream was from God, it was also a dream of guidance. Warnings and guidance overlap. God has not intended for dreams to be messengers of unchangeable calamity or tragedy. That which is seen in a dream is designed to assure our hearts that we will not be destroyed. Even in the Old Testament dreams were aimed at diverting men's paths from the pit (see Job 33:14-18)!

In that dream of judgment, God told Abimelech to approach a saint, the prophet Abraham, who would pray for him. Abimelech had already put himself in harms way. God did not do that. God gave Abimelech a way out of premature death through a dream. In addition, Abraham's marriage was restored and God's plan to bring forth Isaac through Sarah remained intact.

Prophet Abraham was expected to take his place in prayer standing between Abimelech and the harvest of trouble. This is what a saint should do. Saints who are well instructed in God's Word and who know the heart of God do not use prayer to hasten destruction of human lives believing that it is God raining down judgment.

Then thou scarest me with dreams, and terrifiest me through visions:
Job 7:14

Job assumed that the scary dreams and visions that he had during the time of his troubles were from God. God-given dreams do not terrify saints for God does not send a spirit of fear (2 Tim 1:7). It is satan who operates through the spirit of fear. If fear comes to you dressed in dream-language do not treat the dream as a sanctifed dream! Job was one of those people who say, "Things have come to pass just as I dreamt". The truth is that those things have come to pass just as you feared! (see Job 3:25).

It is not scriptural for a believer to have a dream of judgment and then proceed to pray for its fulfillment.

Prioritise the Inward Witness

He has spoken by His son

God, who at sundry times and in divers manners spake in time past unto the fathers by the prophets, Hath in these last days spoken unto us by his Son, whom he hath appointed heir of all things, by whom also he made the worlds;

Hebrews 1:1-2

God is a speaking spirit. He is a revealing God.

God speaks in a variety of ways because we are at different stages of maturity. In the Old Testament, by and large, He supplied spectacular guidance mostly externally. This is because God was relating with spiritually dead people. These various methods by which God spoke could never give the full picture; they were fragmentary.

After the resurrection of Jesus, Cornelius who was not a Christian, saw a spiritual vision before he ever heard the Gospel preached to him. Therefore, one does not need to be a Christian in order to see a genuine vision from the Lord. Visions therefore cannot be a hallmark of deep piety or spirituality. Seeing a vision in and of itself does not even confirm that the one seeing it is a Christian. Cornelius still needed to hear of what Christ had done in order for him to experience the will of God. The full picture, the A to Z, is in the face of Christ Jesus, for Christ is the full expression of God's total will. He is God's communion with us.

The human spirit is the candle

The spirit of man is the candle of the LORD, searching all the inward parts of the belly.
Proverbs 20:27

According to the bible, the real you, your human spirit, is the candle that the Lord uses to guide and bring you His answers in life. In the New Birth that candle is lit by God. What the spirit of the born again one communicates always agrees with God's Word and is never against it. The reason why men find it hard to respond to the leadings of God is because of the way we exercise our wills. Christians also have a will, therefore we improve in our ability to perceive God's leading. God bears witness with my spirit that I am a child of God. A spiritually immature one, a child, has this witness but does nothing with it. A mature one knows this witness and gets led by it. We must not think that God is more faithful to lead the more mature saint than He is faithful to lead the immature one.

The Word of God is the highest spiritual substance that makes us more aware of His thoughts by influencing our will. If we think the Word, we are thinking spiritual thoughts as well as letting our wills align with God's will in our daily walk. As a result we become more aware of the flow of spirit-to-spirit transfer already occurring between our spirits and the Spirit of God.

Our spiritual perception is shaped by our dominant thoughts and influenced by our will. These dominant thoughts either reinforce God's leadings to us or cancel them out. We don't perceive all that God is saying because of the quality of our thoughts.

There is also a spirit-to-soul transfer that helps us understand the revelation that God has already placed into our lives. In order for this understanding to crystallize, peace must be in the heart. Meditating upon the Word causes peace to flow into your heart.

The way peace works is described in Colossians 3:15.

Let peace rule

Let the peace of Christ [the inner calm of one who walks daily with Him] be the controlling factor in your hearts [deciding and settling questions that arise]. To this peace indeed you were called as members in one body [of believers]. And be thankful [to God always]. Colossians 3:15 (Amplified).

God leads us from inside out and not from outside in.

The things of God are confirmed within us as supernatural peace.

We are to let God's peace rule in our heart. God will not push us aside and force upon us the right choices. We have a will with which we allow God's peace have its place in us.

The peace of God is to rule in the heart of man, just like an umpire rules over a game. Contentious situations will arise in the course of the game but everyone gives in to the referee's call. This settles all disputes. Responding to God's peace is how we stay out of trouble in life. This inward witness will give you a "Yes" or "No" about the dreams that you dream as well as everything else in life. Whether or not you know that it is there, the inward witness will always be present. The challenge is, will you override it or be governed by it?

He that believeth on the Son of God hath the witness in himself: he that believeth not God hath made him a liar; because he believeth not the record that God gave of his Son.
1 John 5:10

The way that you obtain inner confirmation that you are now a Christian is through the inward witness. It is the inward witness that makes the New Covenant the dominant thing that it is.

This witness flows out of God's life within the recreated human spirit. It registers as peace and joy in the heart of the born again one. This inward witness is a layer of safety that the believer has in a way that those who lived under the Old Testament did not have, for they were spiritually dead.

And immediately when Jesus perceived in his spirit that they so reasoned within themselves, he said unto them, Why reason ye these things in your hearts?
Mark 2:8

Notice that the Lord Jesus perceived in His spirit while the people around him reasoned within their hearts. We also perceive with our human spirits. In the Christian, our spirits react to whatever we expose it to, in a way that causes it to give us signals which we interpret to get a "Yes" or "No" in life. This inward witness is not fireworks or some gruff voice in the clouds. It is actually not a voice.

There is something close to this in the natural man. It is that which the world refers to as a hunch. In reality, the sinner operates by the reasoning of their hearts.

And Paul, earnestly beholding the council, said, Men and brethren, I have lived in all good conscience before God until this day.
Acts 23:1

The only reason why Paul could have said that he had lived in good conscience before God while murdering the Christians was because of the nature of the human conscience. The conscience of an unbeliever is spectacularly unreliable. Religious zeal had coloured his conscience.

It is your conscience that condemns you when you do not walk in the light of the Word. God does not condemn you. He gives you confidence through His Word. You do not disregard your conscience. You use the Word to train your conscience and then you follow your conscience as it agrees with the Word.

Paul learnt to live in good conscience after he received eternal life and became born again. This conscience becomes more reliable as a man receives God's materiality and feeds his soul on the Word.

There is a difference between conscience and the inward witness. Conscience lets us know the rightness or wrongness of a course of action. The conscience can be defiled if we don't walk in its revelation (see 1 Cor. 8:7). The conscience can be weak. It often has strong ideas where God is silent. This means that conscience is really our sensation of our level of spiritual knowledge. I can sense through my conscience that eating meat is right while you sense that eating the same meat is wrong! This really is not the inward witness. Conscience is more of the soul than the human spirit. We can train the spiritual sensations by changing our level of knowledge.

As Christians we train our conscience by feasting on the realities of redemption. It is the knowledge of what Christ has done that frees your conscience from mysticism and traditions of men.

Spiritual sensations

And it came to pass, as he sat at meat with them, he took bread, and blessed it, and brake, and gave to them. And their eyes were opened, and they knew him; and he vanished out of their sight. And they said one to another, Did not our heart burn within us, while he talked with us by the way, and while he opened to us the scriptures?
Luke 24:30-32

Something happened in them **when He spoke**. Each of these disciples recognized it as a burning sensation that they experienced in their heart.

The bible would usually concentrate on the content of what Jesus said. Here, we are given a glimpse from the perspective of His hearers. We are given unusual insight into the effect that Jesus' words had on the disciples as they listened to him. This is so we know how to interpret the effect of His Word on our heart as we hear His leadings.

On the road to Emmaus, what was that sensation that caused the disciples to say, "did not our heart burn when he spoke?"

Their heart reacted by producing a discernable sensation when exposed to the truth. This sensation was distinct from the way that they had reacted to anything before. It was a welcoming signal. It signified that things were right.

The heart of man reacts to spiritual information and receives sensations from the human spirit.

This burning sensation was a witness from within them of the validity of what Jesus was saying to them and teaching them. This is the primary function of what is called the inward witness. It is how we know that what we are hearing is right or wrong.

What was special was not that their hearts burned but that they each were able to pick up these different shades of heart sensations. They were that sensitive because they had been exclusively with Jesus. Setting out time for God's Word and prayer increases our awareness of these sensations. When spiritual sensations are indistinct to others, they are very real to you.

Once a man receives eternal life, the Holy Spirit bears witness with his spirit that he is a son of God. It is like your own personal pillar of fire by night and pillar of cloud by day only that it is not external. It abides within. That inward anointing was teaching each of these disciples the truth concerning what Jesus was saying to them.

It was not immediately obvious to them why **their hearts burned** within. It was later that they were able to correctly interpret it. The inward witness is to be interpreted and we get better at interpreting it with time. It develops over a period. People are often too hasty to let the inward witness develop fully in them until its message is clear.

But as touching brotherly love ye need not that I write unto you: for ye

yourselves are taught of God to love one another.
1 Thessalonians 4:19

The second most important sensation of the inward witness is that it prompts us on how to correctly walk in love towards other believers in any given situation in which we find ourselves. Walking in love helps us yield more to our recreated spirits. The inward witness is the barometer of the faith walk. When we abandon this, we often shipwreck our faith (see 1 Tim 1:19).

The third most important sensation of the inward witness is the desire within us to pray for others, as we fellowship with God. Some refer to this as the prayer burden.

It is also by the inward witness that boldness is sensed to take dominion over circumstances. This was the groan within Jesus at the tomb of Lazarus. This was a spirit sensation impressed upon the Lord Jesus to take charge and reverse death. It was an inward resistance to the status quo of unbelief and ignorance (see John 11).

Another sensation of the inward witness was that which was at work when the Lord Jesus was troubled in His spirit (see John 13:21). It is like an early warning system that warns of danger ahead. It was by this sensation that the Lord Jesus knew way ahead of time that things were about to get nasty with His own inner circle of disciples. Through this sensation, there is an impartation of an inner resolve to press on, no matter what. Jesus sharpened this through prayer in Gethsemane. This sensation is like setting your alarm to wake you up in the morning.

It is also by the inward witness that you sense that inner provocation to unleash. It is like spiritual adrenalin to take action like Paul did. It is like a spiritual excitement to act. It is that stirring that **precedes ministering the Word of God** (see Acts 17:16).

This is the most overridden sensation of the inward witness. It is that inward sensation that accompanies the inspiration or urge to prophesy. It can be easily explained away. It can be quenched.

Luke also describes another variant of this sensation of the inward witness, when describing Paul's experience in Corinth. He said Paul was "pressed in the spirit". It registers within as a more intense sense of provocation. The sense of urgency is much stronger. By this we understand that the inward witness can be sensed in varying degrees of urgency and intensity.

As we stay full of the Word and give ourselves to prayer, we are able to sense the varying shades of intensity in the impressions that showcase the inward witness of the spirit. We would expect similar combination of sensations to register within us in our daily lives.

Teaches you all things

These things have I written unto you concerning them that seduce you. But the anointing which ye have received of him abideth in you, and ye need not that any man teach you: but as the same anointing teacheth you of all things, and is truth, and is no lie, and even as it hath taught you, ye shall abide in him.
1 John 2:26-27

There is no lie in the inward witness. It is worth noting that the more spectacular the method of communion is, the easier it is for satan to imitate. The devil can tamper with our dreams by sending lying dreams but he cannot tamper with the inward witness; for it flows out from the spirit of a recreated man.

The inward witness is a manifestation of this anointing that we have received of God. This anointing is not a lie. It is how we know what is wrong or right, especially when combating deception.

Some folks are picking up the desires of the flesh but they think that it is the inward witness. There is a difference between fleshly desires and the inward witness. Fleshly "impressions" are rushed and hasty while the inward witness of the spirit is firm, patient and peaceable. If your interpretation of a dream boils down to Apostle Peter telling you to abandon your family and run off with your hot, bible-quoting secretary, and you sense peace about that, such peace does not proceed from the inward witness. It is ungodly, fleshly and unscriptural.

No one starts out an expert in perceiving this witness. We improve as we walk in the light. While we are not to ask God for dreams, we should actively expect to be led primarily through the inward witness.

Inward witness and detailed knowledge

The inward witness is not detailed impartation of knowledge. It is spiritual sensations and impressions registering on our inside.

We can observe this in Paul's famous journey in a ship;

Now when much time was spent, and when sailing was now dangerous, because the fast was now already past, Paul admonished them, And said unto them, Sirs, I perceive that this voyage will be with hurt and much damage, not only of the lading and ship, but also of our lives. Nevertheless the centurion believed the master and the owner of the ship, more than those things which were spoken by Paul. And because the haven was not commodious to winter in, the more part advised to depart

thence also, if by any means they might attain to Phenice, and there to
winter; which is an haven of Crete, and lieth toward the south west and
north west. And when the south wind blew softly, supposing that they had
obtained their purpose, loosing thence, they sailed close by Crete.
Acts 27:9-13

Based on their intimate understanding of the natural laws governing sailing, all the experts agreed that it was a good time to sail. Though Paul did not have their level of expertise, his spirit knew things that the minds of the experts did not know. The centurion paid attention to Paul but he paid far more attention to the experts. People find it easier to listen to you if you were an expert.

There was no verse of scripture that would have given Paul that specific detail about whether to sail or not to sail.

The inward sensations and perceptions of the inward witness are our greatest help in that type of scenario. We get better in giving the uttermost attention to this inward system of sensations and impressions; for it is vital to our life as Christians.

When Paul said, "I perceive", he was not describing something intellectual. He was giving voice to a sensation of the inward witness. A perception is very much like a leading. It is not a Doctoral thesis or a detailed feasibility report. Through this perception or inward witness, Paul knew that there would be danger to the voyage as well as damage to the cargo, the ship itself and the human lives. Paul did not say that God told him this, nor did he say an angel of the Lord told him. Paul had not seen a vision. He just said, "I perceive". That was not God telling him anything.

The inward witness itself would not have been a voice. It would not have literally said, "Paul, this journey will be troublesome".

The inward witness is not vocal. It is not voices or sounds. Paul would have had his internal alarm bells go off. His human spirit would have conveyed a sense that they were about to embark upon something that they shouldn't.

When Paul verbalized that sensation, he was summarizing his conclusions of what the inward witness meant. That statement itself was not the inward witness. It was his understanding of what was being witnessed by his human spirit. As we mature in our walk with God and His Word, we get better in our ability to put into words that which we already knew by an inward perception of the recreated spirit.

It is our interpretation of the inward witness that imparts information. We can have a correct impression but wrong interpretation. It is through meditation on God's Word, walking in love and praying a lot in tongues that we become better at correctly understanding the messages contained within the inward witness. Meditation and tongues are like a spiritual gym. When we pray in tongues our human spirit is actually doing something (1 Cor. 14:14). We are activating the mind of Christ.

We need the peace of God in our minds, in order to function as godly beings on this earth (Phil. 4:7). We are to continually think upon the Word, as this aids the transfer of peace from our spirits to our soul (Phil 4:8). Anxiety and worldliness cause our souls to be a hindrance instead of a help to our spirits and the Holy Spirit.

It is the absence of peace in the heart that causes Christians to be spiritually dull. Everything else hinges on peace. Christians who do not prioritize peace in their hearts, and yet want to perceive God's directions, are like people receiving a text message on a phone whose screen is shattered. The message is already given by God and lodged within the human spirit. The challenge is in perceiving or recognizing it through the soul.

The inward witness is not the same thing as the inward voice of the human spirit. The inward voice is when the human spirit actually passes thoughts and pictures to the soul. The human spirit is saying something to the soul through these thoughts. These are not thoughts originating in our soul. They are the thoughts flowing from our human spirit because it has the life of God. The inward voice of the human spirit is like a dialogue. It is more persuasive than the inward witness. It reacts and responds to our soulish thoughts and reasoning. What Peter experienced in Acts 11:12 and what Paul experienced in Acts 16:6 is not the inward witness or the inward voice of the human spirit. That is the inward voice of the Holy Spirit which is a more intense operation than the inward voice of the human spirit. The inward voice of the Holy Spirit comes across more authoritatively and it carries a stronger sensation of the presence and power of God. The hearer thinks it is external and that others who are present heard the voice. (Acts 8.29, 11:12, 16:6)

Paul treated the inward witness as a reliable guide. He was so developed in it that he addressed others on the back of what he had perceived.

On this particular journey in Acts 27, the experts who could only go by the evidences of the natural world said that every indicator supported sailing on that day. Notice that though Paul heard what these experts said, he remained conscious of his own inner expert – the inward witness. He had an inward perception of danger.

Paul had learnt to pay attention to the inward witness. He had developed his awareness of it much earlier in his life. This made it easier for him to know the meaning of the sensation he perceived in the midst of that crisis. Trying to develop the inward witness when you are going through a crisis tends to backfire. The events of Acts 27 prove that Paul's perception through the inward witness was accurate. Though the experts had said it was OK to go ahead and sail, Paul who was not an expert sailor knew by his inward witness that was not the right course of action.

That inner peace was not putting a stamp of approval on the journey. His spirit was making a call to put a halt to the trip and he knew it. It was a sense of being grieved in his spirit. Something was about to happen that should not happen.

This is available for every Christian.

We will never graduate out of the classroom of following this inward peace.

> *But after long abstinence Paul stood forth in the midst of them, and said, Sirs, ye should have hearkened unto me, and not have loosed from Crete, and to have gained this harm and loss. And now I exhort you to be of good cheer: for there shall be no loss of any man's life among you, but of the ship. For there stood by me this night the angel of God, whose I am, and whom I serve, Saying, Fear not, Paul; thou must be brought before Caesar: and, lo, God hath given thee all them that sail with thee. Wherefore, sirs, be of good cheer: for I believe God, that it shall be even as it was told me. Howbeit we must be cast upon a certain island.*
> *Acts 27:21-26*

If everyone had listened to Paul's perception at the beginning, there would be no economic loss. The loss was not God's plan. It was needless.

Later, God spoke to Paul through a more spectacular means. An angel of the Lord gave Paul the message. Paul was not more confident as a result of the angel speaking to him than he was when all he had was a perception to go by. An inward witness is actually superior to being addressed by an angel of the Lord.

If your dream appears to be saying something, it is by that inward perception of peace that you know what you should really do in line with God's Word. The inward witness will impress upon you certain lines of action to abandon, when you are trying to act upon some dreams. We learn not to override the prompting of the inward witness. We obey the inward witness no matter what.

The inward witness is not a lazy system where you supposedly leave it to God to do your thinking for you. He gave us a mind for a reason. If you have a dream that you feel is significant, judge it by your knowledge of God's Word to see if it agrees with God's Word or if it violates it. Then set yourself in a position to take a stand. At that point, you must perceive the inward witness.

Some facts to remember

This is the third time I am coming to you. In the mouth of two or three witnesses shall every word be established.
2 Corinthians. 13:1

When we have agreement between the inward witness of peace and joy and the Word of God on a matter, we are in safe waters.

To the law and to the testimony: if they speak not according to this word, it is because there is no light in them.
Isaiah 8:20

The written Word of God supplies light in addition to the inward witness of peace and joy. God is behind His Word the same way He is behind the inward witness. You cannot have an inward witness that will contradict the principles of God's written Word or the character of God as seen in His Word.

Notice that God's Word is so supernatural that each one of us is able to get a revelation of his or her own part from meditating on the Word of God (see Rev. 22:19). God is able to quicken portions of His Word to us that we can use to discover God's will for each of our lives. The inward witness will always agree with the Word of God.

God-given dreams are always secondary to God's Word and to the inward witness.

God-given dreams do not contradict the plain teachings of God's Word.

God-given dreams would produce peaceable fruit. It would not promote strife, schisms and withdrawal from the body of Christ.

God-given dreams communicate consistent instruction. If what is communicated keeps changing, in all likelihood, it is not God-given. Sometimes people perceive something and they think God is the one saying it. Perceptions improve with time, whereas God does not improve.

God-given dreams do not violate the principle of divine love as spelt out in 1 Corinthians 13.

While there is no limit to the channels through which God can lead His people, we are not to be one of those Christians who desire for God to talk to them in some audible voice or otherwise through some portent, fleeces or other spectacular means.

God is a spirit and His communications are spiritual. His materiality is in us His children and He wants to discuss with us on a spiritual plane. We are to become spirit conscious since God talks to us spirit to spirit. This is not as spectacular but it is every bit supernatural. It is of God.

Spirit to spirit communication via the inward witness requires faith. It requires a higher level of faith than when we have spectacular communication.

Having God-given dreams and hearing the inward voice of the Holy Spirit are spectacular operations. In the bible, they did not happen everyday. This was not the norm in the church and it won't be the norm in your own life for you to hear God's authoritative voice daily. It was rare then and it will be rare today. It is not a mark of spirituality and you should not seek after it. If these rare operations occur they will always be subject to the Word and the inward witness.

The inward voice in Peter's life

Peter fell into a type of vision that is referred to as a trance (Acts 10:10). In a trance, one is partially or fully unaware of the physical realm. People sometimes fall over bodily when in a trance (see Daniel 10:8-9).

The authoritative voice of the Holy Ghost gave those commands, "Get up, Peter. Kill and eat!" (see Acts 10:13)

The conscience of Peter said, "No way, Lord, for I've never eaten anything profane and unclean." (see Acts 10:14)

Peter's argument with the Lord would imply that he was not conscious of the inward witness on this matter.

The authoritative voice of the Spirit comes across as insistent. In this case, it repeated the command three times to Peter (see Acts 10:16).

It was the authoritative voice of the Holy Ghost that said, "Look, three men are searching for you. Now get up, go down, and go with them doubting nothing, for I have sent them." (see Acts 10:19)

That authoritative voice was aware that Peter doubted (Acts 10:17). Peter doubted the implications of what the authoritative voice of the Spirit was telling him. Through the authoritative voice of the Spirit, God did not tell Peter about every aspect of his life. He did not even address other areas where Peter needed to shape up. The inward voice of the Holy Spirit tends to address specifics. God is not going to dictate to you what you are going to do with every single aspect of your life. God expects you to use His Word, for every aspect of your life.

The scriptures do not tell us whether Peter had an inward witness about that instruction to go with the men from Cornelius or not.

When Peter got to Cornelius' house, he was not too sure what he needed to do but that did not stop him from going. The Spirit did not tell Peter to preach but brought Peter in contact with those who needed to hear the Gospel.

The inward voice in Ananias' life

In a vision, the Lord Jesus by the authoritative voice of the Spirit, told Ananias, "Arise go into the street named straight and inquire in the house of Judas for one called Saul, of Tarsus: for behold he prayeth." (Acts 9:10).

The conscience of Ananias answered, "Lord, I have heard by many of this man, how much evil he hath done to thy saints at Jerusalem:" (Acts 9:13)

Ananias' argument with the Lord would imply that he was not conscious of the inward witness on this matter.

We notice that in both of these instances Peter and Ananias were not planning to take the steps they ended up taking. It was not on their agenda. They had not been paying attention to the inward witness on the matter therefore the inward voice was not confirming something that they already purposed to do. The authoritative voice of the Holy Spirit brought forth a fresh course of action.

When Peter heard the inward voice, it was because the Lord wanted the same outpouring that came upon the Jews to come upon the non-Jews.

When Ananias heard the inward voice, it was because the Lord wanted to bring Saul into the fold of the believers in that town.

In each instance, acting upon the inward voice of the Spirit was instrumental in accomplishing God's plan on the earth.

If God chooses to communicate His plan to you through His inward voice, it is still your responsibility to discern whether it is God's voice. Hearing the inward voice of the Holy Spirit always furthers the plan of God. Almost as important is the fact that it brings benefit to others and not just the one who heard the authoritative voice. In addition, it significantly alters the direction of your life or the lives of those you minister to as a result of it. If what you heard lacks these qualities, it stands to reason that you haven't heard God. Once you confirm that it is God, you are to act on it.

As you meditate on the Word, walk in love and pray in tongues that which is not of the spirit gets mortified. It wanes. Fleshly dreams lose their bite and the appeal of those types of dreams diminishes greatly.

You sow to the spirit by prioritizing and doing the witness of the spirit and the Word (Gal 6:8).

Dreams are a more spectacular form of leading than the written Word and the inward witness but this does not mean that dreams are more accurate than the inward witness or the written Word. Dreams are not more supernatural than the inward witness. Revelation through God's Word is more authoritative than that through dreams or any spectacular operation (See 2 Pet. 1:19).

If a leading was to come via any other operation of the Spirit of God, be it the authoritative voice, dreams, visions or any other spectacular operation, the inward witness is the means by which you will prove it.

Dream Sources

We will dream throughout our stay on this earth. Our dreams pick up input from varying, overlapping sources in real life. We are only separating them so that we can understand them better.

Dreams induced by eating habits

Our dreams will come from one of four sources. The first of which is our diet.

It shall even be as when an hungry man dreameth, and, behold, he eateth; but he awaketh, and his soul is empty: or as when a thirsty man dreameth, and, behold, he drinketh; but he awaketh, and, behold, he is faint, and his soul hath appetite: so shall the multitude of all the nations be, that fight against mount Zion.
Isaiah 29:8

There is a perfectly legitimate physical explanation to dreams.

This would perfectly fit those dreams that are hunger or lack induced. It would appear that poverty specially penetrates into the dream life. You would not classify the dreams you have as a result of hunger as God talking to you. Those dreams would be an overflow of the psychological effects of lack.

The bible shows that what we eat or drink has a significant effect on our dreams. We must not overlook this fact. The desire for food is a strong appetite. If you do not control it, you'll yield to excess and it opens up other areas of your life. You are redirecting spiritual power away from your heart and using it to sustain the excess in the stomach; thus not having enough power for the important things of life! In fact, if we don't learn to balance it with the Word of God, uncontrolled eating habits can drain our spiritual sensitivity and weigh down our heart thus robbing our heart of its effectiveness (see Luke 21:34).

What we eat and drink can influence the dreams that we have. The religious mind dislikes that statement because it'll rather attribute every dream to God. The lesson is that just before we run off thinking that the Lord has given us a "message" through our dreams, we need to rule out the effect of the chemicals pouring into our body through our diet.

Just because a fellow dreams and proclaims that God has spoken to him does not mean that God really spoke. He might be experiencing the effect of food, nutritional deficiency or chemical imbalance. These things are so because man is not purely a spirit being. Our bodies and our souls are linked in such a way that the chemicals in our food affect our psyche in complex ways.

Once we have ruled out the effects of over-indulged eating appetite and chemical imbalance, we are left with three options.

The majority will come from ourselves as a playback of our day's activities, then we have God-given dreams and finally dreams as a result of doors that people open to satan.

Dreams as divine conversations

For God speaketh once, yea twice, yet man perceiveth it not. In a dream, in a vision of the night, when deep sleep falleth upon men, in slumberings upon the bed; Then he openeth the ears of men, and sealeth their instruction,
Job 33:14-16

We notice that God-given dreams are here referred to as visions of the night. That is mostly because those that worked did so during the day and otherwise slept at night in bible times. In our day with its plurality of work arrangements and shifts, the vision of the night might as well be a vision of the morning or any part of the day.

God-given dreams will manifest one or a combination of the revelation gifts of the Spirit. It will be the manifestation of the word of knowledge, the word of wisdom, the discerning of spirits or a combination of them.

Dreams do not occupy the same central role in the believer today as it once occupied in the life of the Old Testament people. This is because while they were spiritually dead, we have received life in Christ Jesus and we don't have to sleep in order for God to talk to us.

Notice that it says that God speaks one way and in another. This means that God speaks to people in various ways and He repeats Himself. He speaks in various ways and at different levels because people are at different stages of spiritual awareness and development. When we are not as spirit-conscious as we should be, in His mercy, God does not abandon us. He tries to impress the same warning to us in symbolic form through dreams. The dream serves to arrest our attention as a last resort. Dreams are not on par with getting direction through God's Word and the inward witness.

Though we refer to God-given dreams as spectacular leadings, they are warnings. If God communicates to us through dreams, He is emphasizing to us those warnings that we should have picked up through the inward witness but have not picked up. We sometimes become so engrossed in our course of action that we are no longer walking in the light that we have. When we bypass these primary sources, the avenue of last resort is dreams. In that case, these dreams provide warnings about the things going on in our lives. We get directions from our walk in the light with God. When you examine a dream, you are not looking to harvest directions from it. The idea that He speaks in one way and in two means that He has many ways of speaking to us, of which dreams are a last resort. The inward witness is a higher level of receiving directions from God than dreams are or ever will be.

From the bible, we see that all God-given dreams draw our attention to the future (see chapter 4 & 5). These dreams will use imagery from your past but they hardly ever talk about your past. God-given dreams focus us on the future.

When God transmits into our life in the form of dreams, it is authoritative. It arrests our attention in such a manner that we usually remember it. The exception to this rule was Nebuchadnezzar had a God-given dream and then forgot it afterwards.

Dreams as inner conversations

I will bless the LORD, who hath given me counsel: my reins also instruct me in the night seasons.
Psalm 16:7

We notice that just as counsel flows from the Lord, there are instructions that flow from our own inner life in the night seasons. The night seasons refer to when we sleep. For a person who works night shifts, and sleeps during the day, the day become his night seasons.

When we sleep, our heart rearranges our experiences and presents them to us through our dreams. The abundance in the heart needs to find a vent for expression. The abundance of the heart does not only come forth as words, they show up as dreams. You can use the words of your own mouth to program energy sapping dreams into your life.

The heart of man is a spiritual visual machine. It says to us in picture-form many things that are not too easy to put into words. The dreams from ourselves could be our spirit trying to get a point across to us or trying to grab our attention in an area. Most times though it is our souls trying to give us feedback.

Our heart often speaks to us in ways that no other person is able to. The masks that we put on for others are off and we are face to face with our own thoughts. Education and society groom us to suppress most of this in our everyday life. We are groomed to behave in certain ways and project ourselves in particular ways. We are required to act the part. After a while, we sometimes believe our own hype. Your dreams are a means for your heart to play back its rearrangement of your activities. We have an opportunity to discover where we really are. In that sense, a fellow who believes the worst, entertains toxic thoughts and sows unwise actions could find himself reaping a turbulent and energy-draining dream life. In the same vein, a fellow who watches violent films and consistently has violent dreams is getting feedback from his heart of the effect of those films on the fabric of the soul. Those dreams are not his problems, they are merely symptoms. Such a fellow should submit his soul to God's Word and the Word would change his taste in films while also cleansing his dream life.

The flesh also sends pictures to our soul in the form of temptations. There is nothing gentle about these images or the ferocity with which they come.

For what man knoweth the things of a man, save the spirit of man which is in him? even so the things of God knoweth no man, but the Spirit of God.
1 Corinthians 2:11

Your human spirit knows perfectly about different aspects of your life. Your spirit is equipped to bring you leadership in life because it knows about you perfectly. Dreams could be our spirits revealing things to us that we should be dealing with. This is our spirit imparting instructions to our soul through images that we become aware of at night, when the carnal mind is not as strong.

The language of the human spirit is visual because spirits commune better with pictures than with spoken words. Though spirits communicate visually and pictures convey better than words, the message contained within these images is often lost on our understanding. Where people do not prioritize the love-walk, the human spirit and soul are at war. Therefore, when their spirits are trying to get something across to them through the visual medium of dreams their fleshly interpretations muddle it up. Dreams that are wrongly interpreted are also inevitably wrongly applied. As we prioritise the love-walk and feed on the Word, we renew our minds and find that we are better able to make meaning of our dreams.

We don't obtain guidance from these dreams as final authority. As Christians, God's Word and the Spirit guide us. These dreams are windows from which we can observe the state of our hearts. They are a feedback system.

Our dreams are not always a function of our own spirits. More often than not, they are our spoken words dramatized. They can also flow from the soul realm as it tries to visually play back our beliefs, thoughts and actions to us (see Eccl. 5:3).

For in the multitude of dreams and many words there are also divers vanities: but fear thou God.
Ecclesiastes 5:7

It is a sobering thought that having multitude of dreams does not make the dreamer spiritually minded. They do not increase our reverence for God. It seems that as dreams multiply so does the temptation to speak empty words. It is not a life filled with dreams that causes us to grow up spiritually. People who do not give the Word of God first place tend to attach too much meaning to dreams and get broken trying to use dreams to sort out things that they should use the Word for. Dreams are not a substitute for God's Word. We are to base our lives on the Word of God and learn to fill our thoughts and our words with God's Word.

Writing down your dreams

One must know how to write dreams down for later meditation. Daniel who was a man of excellence and a serious student of the supernatural wrote down his dreams. We should strive for excellence in these things too.

In the first year of Belshazzar king of Babylon Daniel had a dream and visions of his head upon his bed:
Daniel 7:1

Notice that Daniel wrote down the setting. It was in the first year of King of Belshazzar. This gives enough background information. It must have been a time of great change for him, for it was the first year of a new king. That immediately allows Daniel to relate it to a certain portion in his life. Apparently, Daniel did not have this dream while he was in someone's house or when he was on vacation. It was the "visions of his head upon his bed". This hints at the remote possibility that through our souls, we can tap into the experiences of others. In much the same way that I can smell your perfume if I hold your cloth close to my nose, it is possible to pick up the emotions, feelings and fears of others, when we are in their presence. None of the things experienced describe you. You are experiencing your sensitivity to someone else's experiences. These things could register in our dreams. We must not then assume that it is God talking to us or saying anything to us.

Both Apostles Peter and Jude imply that the flesh can give us dreams (see Jude 1:8, 2 Peter 2:10). If you continually yield to your flesh and keep giving in to its lusts, the flesh will generate lots of filthy dreams. Filthy dreamers do not believe the best about others but think the worst of them when awake. This continues in their dreams. They often declare these to be spiritual warfare or prophetic dreams. In reality, their dreams are a theatre for the flesh.

If you indulge your flesh, you would likely suffer for it in your dream life. God is not punishing anyone with those dreams.

They are reaping troublesome dreams from the flesh. People who do not prioritise the love-walk and the Word have no defence against fleshly dreams. Fleshly dreams don't announce themselves with glowing neon signs. We are to increase our love-walk and make no provision for the flesh, to fulfil the lusts (see Rom. 13:14).

Dreams from satan

Since God does not send a spirit of fear (2 Tim 1:7), the scary dreams and visions that Job had during the time of his troubles were from satan who attacked him through the spirit of fear. Satan uses these dreams to deceive people into opposing themselves as well as fighting others. It is a product of fear. Perfect love casts out such fear (1 John 4:18).

The bible says very little about nightmares.

Classification of dreams

Joel's prophecy concerning the church age implies that a radical shift has come to the dream life of the people of God.

A careful study of scriptures shows that dreams come in two broad varieties.

Dreams that use symbols

Majority of our dreams make use of parables. In these parables, one thing represents something else, therefore, they require interpretation. For example, the dreams of Pharaoh's Chief Baker and Chief Butler were symbolic. The symbols contained within your dreams mean to you things that it does not mean to another. It is easier to dream a dream than to interpret it. A knife to a surgeon does not mean the same thing to a thug. For one, it is a means of peace; while for the other, it is the mechanism of strife. You would quickly get confused if you discussed your dream with 10 different people. Each would likely give you 10 different interpretations and you would not be any wiser than when you started out. Symbolic dreams are the hardest to master. Many mismanage them to their own detriment. Joseph was able to interpret other people's dreams because he had a God-given gift for interpreting dreams.

Pharaoh's dreams in Genesis 40 were symbolic in nature. Pharaoh had two dreams in one night, each following the other in succession. He was visualizing one dream two different ways for emphasis and detail. Thankfully, Pharaoh was smart enough to know that God was not telling him about a new breed of carnivorous cattle waiting to be discovered.

Dreams that don't use symbols

Each of Joseph's recorded dreams was a direct encounter with the Angel of the Lord who brought him messages at important points in the life of Jesus, while Jesus was a child. It was through these dreams that he knew about the role that he was to play. All of Joseph's recorded dreams occurred in the very early years of Jesus. Afterwards, we have no record of Joseph or his dreams.

Joseph's dreams were clear and direct, totally lacking in symbols. They were direct instructions about what his next steps were. Joseph could get up in the morning and act on what he had seen. The chances of missing the interpretation were nearly zero.

The directed message from the angel was, "fear not to take unto thee Mary thy wife:" Matthew 1:20

At another time it was, Arise, and take the young child and his mother, and flee into Egypt," Matthew 2:13

Those were direct instructions not requiring any interpretation.

Joseph would have needed to understand that his dreams were not symbolic but actual impartation of information as a result of interacting with an Angel. Both the Angel and the instruction to flee into Egypt were not symbolic. Joseph would have caused himself untold harm had he treated that dream as symbolic. He would likely say that Egypt represents the world. In which case, he was receiving instruction to run into the world? He had received a direct instruction to migrate to Egypt for a while.

Sometimes this type of dream is given in story form. The main message is within the story itself. The summary is the meaning. We are not given the exact details of the dream that the wise men had. They likely saw many things in their dreams but they understood that the core message of that dream was that it was a warning not to return to Herod. The details of the dream are not as important as the message it carries. This is not really an interpretation but ability to separate the core from the story.

And a vision appeared to Paul in the night; There stood a man of Macedonia, and prayed him, saying, Come over into Macedonia, and help us. And after he had seen the vision, immediately we endeavoured to go into Macedonia, assuredly gathering that the Lord had called us for to preach the gospel unto them.
Acts 16:9-10

Some scholars have pointed out that it was at Troas that Luke joined Paul's ministry team. Up till this point in his record of Acts, Luke had been reporting everything in the third person. It is here, for the first time that the narrative shifts from "them" to "we".

Paul had tried severally to take the gospel to different places but the Holy Spirit did not permit him. It was during this period that he had a vision of the night. A vision of the night is very much like a God-given dream. In the night vision, Paul heard the man from Macedonia saying, "Come over to Macedonia". It is almost like a commentary letting Paul know assuredly what the dream meant. It would appear that a night vision is easier to interpret than a dream.

A tiny but important detail in that dream was that it was a man of Macedonia that told Paul to come. Paul concluded that he should minister among the Macedonians. Philippi was the chief city of that section of Macedonia (see Acts 16:12).

Paul and Silas had seen a vision of doing ministry in Macedonia. They had not seen a trip to the jail though they ended up there! You don't release your faith for persecution. Wicked and unreasonable men guarantee that.

At midnight, Paul and Silas set their will to praise God in such a loud voice that the other prisoners heard them. They were not praising God in order that the prison doors might be opened. They were just letting God know that they loved Him. A consequence of this was that such power was released through their praise that it caused a localised earthquake. Most people would have escaped after an earthquake freed them from prison. Especially since they were jailed under false and trumped up charges; there is nothing wrong with escaping in such circumstances. Amazingly, Paul and Silas would not escape nor would the other prisoners who had witnessed the whole thing. They were filled with the awe of God. I think Paul did not leave because he had not yet ministered to the man he had seen in the vision.

Luke gives us some interesting detail.

The keeper of the jail called for light for the whole episode had played out in darkness. I believe that Paul must have seen the keeper's face through the illumination of that light as he fell trembling before Paul and Silas. It is likely that this was the man of Macedonia that had appeared to Paul in the night vision. Paul finally had his man!

Paul got the chance to minister to the keeper of the jail and his entire household; they all became Christians together, who had heard the message and believed in the Lord Jesus. This was the start of the Philippian church.

The Philippian church became the major sponsors of Paul's ministry. It all started by Paul properly interpreting and applying a God-given vision of the night.

Prophetic dreams

If there arise among you a prophet, or a dreamer of dreams, and giveth thee a sign or a wonder
Deuteronomy 13:1

There is a diversity within the prophet's office. Old Testament Prophets were sometimes referred to as dreamers of dreams. These dreams were on a ministerial level, accompanied with a higher anointing upon them. It was really the gift of the discerning of spirits at work. They were seeing into the spirit realm. These prophets received their prophetic utterance in visual form, for they were seers. A seer is a prophet who hears by seeing visions. All seers are prophets but not all prophets are seers (see 1 Chron. 29:29).

These prophetic dreams are as a result of the anointing upon interacting with our dream life. This anointing amplifies the dream as a result of which they come across with greater clarity.

Getting ready to interpret

Though a lot has been written about dream interpretation in both the secular and religious press, much of what the scriptures reveal about interpreting our dreams have been ignored!

Whether a dream proceeds from our soul, our spirit or from God's Spirit, most of our dreams would tend to have a strong element of a parable to them since they involve symbols.

Anything that involves symbols is subject to interpretation. Our accuracy improves with experience. Without a doubt, we can improve in our ability to interpret our dreams.

There are those who see every element in our dreams as a representation of our emotions. Thus according to that school of thought, if you dream of entering into a dark forest full of wild animals, they would see the forest as jumbled up emotions. They would propose that the various animals represent various emotions vying for our attention. Therefore, they would see the dream as saying that we are struggling in our emotions and trying to achieve balance.

I Daniel was grieved in my spirit in the midst of my body, and the visions of my head troubled me. I came near unto one of them that stood by, and asked him the truth of all this. So he told me, and made me know the interpretation of the things.
Daniel 7:15-16

Even though Daniel was a prophet who saw visions, he recognised that seeing a vision is only one side of the coin when it comes to visions. He knew when the meaning eluded him. He did not force a meaning. Being available to receive a vision does not imply that the vision is understood. Smart people don't force meanings upon their dreams or visions. They also know that it is more important to know the meaning of a dream than to dream it in the first instance.

After Pharaoh dreamt, he said, "And I told it to the magicians, but there was no one who could explain it to me." (Gen 41:24)

We must be very careful when reading the Old Testament.

Just because an episode is written in the bible does not make it a scriptural example to follow.

It is perfectly understandable that Pharaoh approached magicians for help; after all Pharaoh was a street-wise son of wrath who dined with the devil. A Christian does not go to magicians. It is magicians that should seek the Christian, so the saint can help clarify the magician's confusion; for we are the light of the world.

While it should not be the case, it appears that majority of people find themselves responding towards God-given dreams like Pharaoh. They know that they have had a significant dream but do not know how to unpack it in order to harvest its meaning.

Pharaoh was actually spiritually smarter than most saints are today. He knew when the explanation of a dream did not satisfy him. Today, too many saints accept the first explanation that anyone attempts. Just because a notable magician has interpreted a dream does not mean that that explanation should be satisfactory to you. In the first instance, a saint should know what his own dream means, if its meaning should be explored at all.

God is not the only source of dreams

One of the most important concepts to understand in relation to dreams is that God is not the only source of dreams. Dreams could also arise from our activities, or the operations of the enemy.

We have a divinely assigned responsibility to test all things, distinguish between the things that differ and hold fast to that which is true. Just because you dreamt does not mean that the dream is from God.

Don't undo what Christ has done

We must not interpret our dreams in ways that mock the finished works of Christ or toss away our precious redemption, as though it was an afterthought. We should not entertain interpretations that belittle what Christ has accomplished.

The saints interpreted their own dreams

Ordinarily as you read through scriptures, we don't find a single instance of a covenant person going to another person in order to get the interpretation of their God-given dreams. If the Holy Spirit gives you a dream, He will also give you its interpretation. If you are unable to perceive the interpretation, He would place people within your circle of relationships who understand enough of the context of your life to help you navigate these waters. The truth is that the anointing within is able to teach you enough to unravel the meaning of any dream you have. Whatever happens, do not become anxious because you have a dream whose interpretation you don't yet perceive.

Without a doubt, there were many instances where one man sought the help of another in order to get the interpretation of their own dream. We find that these men were not saints. In each instance, they approached saints to do the interpretation. The saints interpret for the sinner and not for another saint. None of those who sought interpretation from another were saints.

Know God's Word & Know Thyself

The Word of God is the mystery that unravels all mysteries. If you have to attach meanings to any symbols, learn to draw your meanings from the bible. As you become full of God's Word, the Word cuts away all the fluff that clutters your dream life. You are able to go into the Word and let the Word bring out the meaning of things for you.

The expression, "beware of dogs", was used by Paul in the bible (Phil 3:2). If you dream about dogs and you have to attach meanings to that (you don't have to by the way), you'll find that the Word uses dogs in two broad senses. The Jews referred to those not included in the Abrahamic covenant as dogs (Mt. 15:26-27). In the epistles, 'dogs' refers to putting confidence in legalism instead of God's grace. It is rejecting the grace of God. Therefore, dogs don't represent something spiritually cool.

If you are a dog trainer, I would expect dogs to show up in your dreams a lot! In that case, I would not attach a spiritual meaning to dogs. For that type of person, dogs in dreams might refer to livelihood. We have to apply scriptural common sense to these things. It matters who saw the dog. Dogs do not have to mean to you what it means to some other person. Always let the Word of God shape your conclusions rather than prioritising your dreams above the Word of God. Our dream life is subject to God, His love and His Word revealed to us. So, the first principle of interpretation of dreams is to know God's Word and to know thyself.

Don't be in a hurry to interpret your dream

Then Daniel, whose name was Belteshazzar, was astonied for one hour, and his thoughts troubled him. The king spake, and said, Belteshazzar, let not the dream, or the interpretation thereof, trouble thee. Belteshazzar answered and said, My lord, the dream be to them that hate thee, and the interpretation thereof to thine enemies.
Daniel 4:19

Daniel, one of the most proficient dream interpreters in all of God's Word, helps us see the principle that we should not be in a hurry to slap a meaning upon a God-given dream, if the meaning is not immediately obvious to us personally.

Though Daniel knew the king, there was the passage of time before Daniel interpreted the king's dream. We know this is the case because after the king finished telling his dream to Daniel, the bible says, "Then Daniel, whose name was Belteshazzar, was astonied for one hour, and his thoughts troubled him". This means it took Daniel at least one hour of meditation to correctly piece together the words that allowed him to communicate the meaning. Daniel avoided giving interpretations in a hurry. This would mean that it is not God's intention that we use church services to give and interpret dreams. Usually, when giving interpretation to a tongue, you give the interpretation immediately afterwards. We must not be pressured into forcing fleshly interpretations to God-given dreams. The end result is tragic.

We do ourselves much damage by trying to cook up an interpretation when we really don't have any. There are some dreams that we suspend in our imagination while we pray in tongues and meditate on God's Word. Not every dream has a meaning or need be given a meaning. Whatever the case, we don't force meanings. The unction from God makes us know what to do.

Beware of a wounded conscience

The bible says, "a dream cometh through the multitude of business" (Eccl 5:3). This means that the cumulative of our beliefs, thoughts and actions have a way of filtering back to you through your dreams. Thus, some of our weird dreams are an exploration of the weirdness of our beliefs, thoughts and actions. It means that your slant in life carries over into your dream.

This means that you unconsciously have indirect control of your dream life by the choices you make in your every-day life.

The important principle involved here is that if our conscience has been wounded, it will show up in our dream life. We can be saved much heart ache if we know how to watch out for it.

If I was silly enough to watch horror movies two nights in a row before going to bed, and I have repeated apocalyptic dreams about the world coming to an end, I would be un-smart if I interpret that to mean the launch of my global prophetic ministry. God is not telling me anything; I have shocked my system into spasms and it is giving me feedback in the form of violent dreams.

We invariably will later reap the bitterness or joy towards others that we let dominate our consciousness, just before we go to bed, as dreams. There is nothing magical about retaining bitterness in our hearts towards someone and then seeing that person try to fight you in your dreams. It is your bitterness holding you to ransom and projecting itself onto your dreams. It does not make the other person diabolical.

If you had an argument with a fellow and see that fellow trying to shoot you with a gun in your dream, it would be unwise to conclude from that dream that God is taking sides with you and showing you the duplicity of that other fellow. Your conscience has been hurt by your interactions with that person. You cannot interpret such dreams to be a revelation that the other fellow is a Mafia boss of the underworld! More likely, the dream tells you how you view the person. No, God is not speaking to you, your biases are! Our emotional biases have a voice. Dreaming that way about a person with whom you have a grudge does not tell you anything about the person. It is not about the person, it is about you. Those dreams tell you that your conscience has been wounded. What you feel about the person has sunk deep into your consciousness. In that sense, such a dream is a help for it tells you attitudes and emotional slants that you need to work on.

We are not quick to jump to conclusions after we have dreamt about others. We first examine our motives and attitudes towards the person, before we assume our dreams are God's prophetic voice to us. Not all dreams are to be treated as God-given dreams.

When a wounded conscience gives us the supernatural "gift of suspicion" which causes us to suspect others, we should prioritise the clear instructions within the Word of God to walk in love towards others above any tendency to become suspicious of them because of a dream.

It is worth remembering that in the overwhelming majority of cases, your dream is about you, even if you see others in your dream. Ask yourself, "What does this person tell me about me?"

Exercise Faith

Daniel was a man who knew how to interpret dreams. From his life we see that we do not earn interpretation of dreams. They are a product of God's grace. They are given as a gift from God.

Release your faith and be fully confident that you will be able to interpret any important dream (see Dan 2:16).

Daniel was a fellow who set his heart to understand (see Daniel 10). He was not the kind of fellow that assumed that if he were meant to know these things he would know it before he dies. He actively pursued it with his faith and expectancy, and so should we. He fasted so as to receive revelation. The fasting and expectancy is not warming up God, it is stirring up Daniel and causing him to rise up to take what the Lord provides.

Nebuchadnezzar forgot his own dream but he still wanted its interpretation. Kings made unusual requests in ancient times. No one in the bible had been given that kind of challenge before. Daniel prayed to God and expected God to replay Nebuchadnezzar's dream to him and God did! God replayed the dream to Daniel while he slept. In a sense, Daniel dreamt Nebuchadnezzar's dream all over again and had enough soundness of mind to remember it all.

If you had a significant dream whose details you forgot, you could pray to God to repeat it for you and God would cause it to come back. It would appear from scriptures that the ability to interpret our own dreams gets better as we exercise faith for it and follow up that expectancy with prayer. During prayer these abilities are imparted as well as stirred up.

Faith for interpreting dreams comes from hearing God's Word in that area. You are to believe that God has given you the interpretation (see Genesis 40:8, Gen 41:16)

Increasing your spiritual sensitivity

It was as Peter was praying that he heard the Lord Jesus speak to him in a vision (see Acts 10:8-17). It was also as Cornelius was praying that the angel spoke to him to send for Peter (see Acts 10:2-3). This shows that asides from communion with God, the real benefit of praying is that it is a way of prioritizing our spiritual senses over our physical senses. Real prayer awakens us to the spirit realm and helps us become more sensitive to God's Spirit.

Prayer is a means of receiving interpretation of dreams. It is also a means of building up yourself to be able to interpret your own dreams, and it aids supernatural recall of dreams that we might otherwise have forgotten.

Lessons from Joseph's Interpretations

Our confidence in interpreting our dreams can be further strengthened as we study some principles that the Word reveals concerning interpretation of dreams in the life of Joseph.

Interpretation of dreams belong to God

Dreams are often communicated in symbolic language; they could therefore come across as weird or silly. Pharaoh's dream of seven thin cows eating up seven fat cows come across as a ridiculous tale, which should be thrown away. That is the case until we read Joseph's interpretation, which makes sense once we hear it.

Joseph's secret to dream interpretation was that he knew that interpretation of dreams belongs to God. He expected God to pass on the interpretation to him by the Holy Spirit. (see Genesis 40:8).

A most fundamental principal to remember about dreams is that they were given to you, they occurred in your sleep and were seen through your own eyes; therefore, they are your dream. They should mean something to you. The reason why you were the one that had the dream is because the Holy Spirit has given you resources, within the supernatural well on your inside, with which to unpack its meaning.

If God was the one who gave you a dream, He is equally able to give you its interpretation. He does not hide the interpretation from you.

In the Old Testament, only a select few had access to the Spirit of God. Today every saint does. If the Holy Spirit has chosen to communicate to you through dreams, He will not give you a dark puzzle that you can only understand by running from pillar to post looking for someone else to interpret it to you.

If you believe that you would attach the wrong interpretation to your dreams, you would be programming your heart to deceive you with futile interpretations.

Your dream draws from your experiences

If God were to communicate to you through a dream, He would involve things that you can relate with. What we see in our dreams reflects us more than it reflects God. Somehow we influence the symbols that are shown to us in our dreams. As our experiences become richer and more varied, so does our dream life. We influence the symbols that will be dominant in our dreams.

Joseph saw sheaves in his early dreams as a teenager.

Pharaoh's Baker saw bread.

Pharaoh's Butler saw cup and wine. This makes sense.

You will notice that Joseph did not see wine in his dream, the Baker did not see sheaves and the Butler did not see bread.

God did not give the Baker or Butler dreams from the perspective of Joseph. The symbols used were from the lives of the dreamers. This means that the symbols in your dream mean something to you and not to those you tell the dream to.

What is shown to each, means something to that individual and ordinarily that individual should be able to interpret it.

Thus, the setting of a dream means something to the dreamer and not to those who hear the dream; although you'll find that the more you relate to a person, the easier it is to interpret their dream or at least get a sense of what their dream is about. We notice that even though Daniel had the God-given ability to interpret dreams, it wasn't a case of Daniel living in Bethlehem trying to interpret the dream of a king who lived in Persia. Daniel knew the king. They were not complete strangers. Ordinarily, we cannot correctly interpret a person's dream if we do not know the context of that person's life. The more we know about that person, the more accurate the dream interpretation becomes. This is why Jacob and his children attempted to interpret Joseph's dreams. They knew Joseph.

And he said unto them, Hear, I pray you, this dream which I have dreamed: For, behold, we were binding sheaves in the field, and, lo, my sheaf arose, and also stood upright; and, behold, your sheaves stood round about, and made obeisance to my sheaf.
Genesis 37:6-7

You will notice that Joseph saw himself doing in his dream that which he did in everyday life – binding sheaves. Personally, I would be surprised if God gave me a dream in which I was binding sheaves. I am not Joseph or Jacob. They were farm owners. I am not yet. God uses what is, to reveal what shall be. Since Joseph bound sheaves in real life, there was nothing spectacular about him binding them in his dream life. The principle that we see here is that our dreams will borrow symbols from our backgrounds and experience. In all likelihood, you would not see yourself landing on the moon in your dreams, if you are not a science fiction writer or an astronaut. This is why we don't find dreams in the bible where the dreamers were in a rocket or space ship – the technology had not been seen or explored by men, nor was it their experience; therefore, it did not show up in their dreams.

I have never raced a mammoth whether in real life or in a computer game, therefore, it would be significant if I found myself dreaming about racing a mammoth at the North Pole.

As a general principle, we would do well to understand how the bible treats certain imagery and symbols. Serpents and dogs are not presented in positive light; therefore, we are wary of them in our dreams if we take those dreams serious at all.

On a general note therefore, snakes in dreams would not represent something cool. However, if I were a snake handler or a student of zoology interacting with snakes as part of my daily research activities, snakes would hold significance to me that they would not for the typical person. Dreaming about snakes after watching a documentary about wildlife is likely a feedback from your soul.

If you saw your pet dog in a dream, it would be foolish to say that represents the Pharisee attitude. Your pet dog means something to you that it does not mean to anyone else. Personally, I don't have a pet dog in real life therefore, I don't expect to see any in my dreams. So if we both saw dogs in our dreams, we should not ordinarily attach the same meaning to them.

Your dream says something about you

We can learn some things from Joseph's dreams in Genesis. We observe that in Joseph's dream, he did not see his brothers nor did he even see himself. Their sheaves represented them in much the same way that Joseph's sheaf represented Joseph. You could say that Joseph was present in that dream as the sheaf that stood up.

Joseph dreamt afterwards and saw the sun, moon and eleven stars bow before him. The second dream was a continuation of the first in which only his brothers were in view. By having the same dream twice the certainty of its fulfilment was being emphasised to him. That second dream was the same message that had been shown previously through the imagery of sheaves. In our dreams, different symbols can be used at different points in our development to emphasise the same thing to us. At one time, it was enough to use sheaves and as Joseph grew in his understanding of his role, the stars of the heavens could be used to represent the same point. The progression from sheaves to stars shows that Joseph was progressing in his understanding of the extent of his rulership.

Thus when Joseph dreamt about sheaves, he was really dreaming about himself. When he dreamt about the sun and the moon, he was dreaming about himself in relation to the members of his family. From this principle, we understand that even if ten thousand people show up in your dream, you are really dreaming about you.

Even when we see others in our dreams, we should not see this as a message about that person. It will definitely be wrong to hold someone responsible in real life for an advice they gave you in your dream! Those people represent characteristics about ourselves that we need to pay attention to. In that sense, your own spirit may show up as your pastor. You know what these things mean by learning to depend on the Greater One within you.

Abimelech's dream was about himself.

The Baker's dream was about himself.

The Butler's dream was about himself.

Joseph dreamt about himself.

If there is a principle for dream interpretation to remember, it is this fact; your dreams say more about you than it says something about anyone else. You might not even show up in your own dream as you!

Daniel emphasized this point to Nebuchadnezzar when he told Nebuchadnezzar, "thou art the head of gold" (see Daniel 2:38)

Thus Nebuchadnezzar was present in his own dream as the head of gold.

Later Nebuchadnezzar dreamt and Daniel says to Nebuchadnezzar, "You are that tree in the midst of the earth" (see Daniel 4:22). Thus Nebuchadnezzar showed up in his own dream not a human being but as a mighty tree! This symbol of a tree represents the fact that Nebuchadnezzar was now well established and strong.

Since your dreams will say something about you, you need to understand that you are the most qualified to interpret your own dreams.

Interpret in line with your sphere of authority

A repeated dream does not necessarily occur in one night. It could be interrupted and return later to continue to completion over a period of days or a longer period. The Word of God within you will make sense of it all.

Pharaoh's dream is one of the most famous dreams that were of the type that was repeated (See Genesis 41).

The very first image of thin cows eating up fat cows already set the core message that God was trying to convey to Pharaoh. This tends to be the case with dreams, which have multiple settings. The first scene gives the subject and the others give detail. The subsequent scenarios simply built on and expanded out the first setting.

In line with the other principles we have seen, the imagery of cow and cattle were measures of wealth to Pharaoh.. The Nile meant life to Pharaoh. Pharaoh's position is such that he is the owner of cows, therefore one that commands wealth. Another Egyptian could have a dream involving cows but if that person were a butcher, the cows would not mean to that person what it means to Pharaoh.

If God wanted to convey information relating to the economy to me today, He would not use a cow. He would use something that represents that information to me.

Take note of the fact that Joseph's interpretation said, "throughout all the land" (see Genesis 41:29). It was the land of Egypt or wherever the dominion of Pharaoh extends to. The scope of Pharaoh's dream was at least national. It applied to the whole kingdom that Pharaoh had control of. Joseph's interpretation shows that the dream was about the economy of Pharaoh's kingdom. God wanted to preserve the lives in that kingdom. The man that could organise all the resources of the kingdom was the Pharaoh himself. It makes scriptural sense that God gave this dream to Pharaoh. God could see that there was global tragedy on the horizon and that Pharaoh did not know it. God expected Pharaoh to get its meaning and take appropriate action. It is staggering the faith that God has in man!

Imagine what confusion would have come about if Joseph had interpreted the Chief Baker's dream to refer to the fate of all the bakers of Egypt? That baker, though he was an important baker, had not dreamt about the execution of all the bakers of the kingdom of Egypt (see Genesis 40). The baker did not have a national influence; therefore, his interpretation should not take on a national significance.

The dreams that we dream are to be interpreted in line with our position and influence in life.

You'll not likely dream about another man's family or what some other person should do.

A God-given dream that repeats itself indicates urgency. It also indicates that there a prophetic nature to the dream about things that will surely come to pass.

God used Joseph's interpretation to bring about his exaltation in Egypt. Some folks want to have nothing to do with this world supposedly because of the evil in it. We are the salt of the earth and the light of our world. Our light is primarily needed in the midst of darkness and not in heaven. It was by faith that Joseph ascended the throne in Egypt. It was also by the same faith that Moses forsook the throne of Egypt (Heb. 11:27). Moses was not better than Joseph. We just have to find out how best to express faith in a given situation in line with God's plan for our lives.

The principle is that our dreams convey to us things within our circle of influence. If my influence was global, then I would dream global dreams. An unknown fellow would not be given a dream about things that are outside his control. Nebuchadnezzar was a world ruler, therefore he dreamt about the world. This means that even if your interpretation were correct, its application would be within the bounds of your influence.

To the pure all things are pure

Another principle we see, is that Joseph interpreted Pharaoh's dream in a way that stirred up the spirit of faith. His interpretation was not fatalistic. The maturity in Joseph was to quickly see that this was a conditional word of wisdom. It was not anything written in the stars. There were things that could be done to cushion the blow of the seven years of scarcity! This then makes this dream a warning dream though everything about it at first glance makes it comes across as inevitable calamity.

You see, to the pure all things are pure. You can tell a person's spiritual health by the way they interpret dreams. Some folks are too gloom and doom minded to be of good to themselves or anyone else. Joseph understood that the dream that Pharaoh had was a word of wisdom about the future. The word of wisdom was over a 14-year period. First, there would be seven years of plenty and afterwards, seven years of scarcity that would erase the memory of the initial years of plenty.

Whereas spiritual intelligence is involved in interpreting a dream, no spiritual intelligence is required to dream it. It definitely takes spiritual intelligence to understand when something is conditional.

It is true that the scarcity was going to come to pass. That was why the dream was repeated. It is not however true that the scarcity was the end of the universe and life as we know it. A warning dream can be prevented. They could not prevent the scarcity but they could prevent the calamity that would have come about as a result of the scarcity by wise planning.

People that subscribe to fatalism would have Pharaoh's type of dream and follow it up accurately with Joseph's type of interpretation and then have a fatalistic application! A fatalistic application is the one that would have said, "Famine is coming and there is nothing we can do about it". A warning dream means we can exercise the authority contained within our humanity and reap a good end result.

Our understanding of the nature of God is key. It determines how we interpret dreams. Pharaoh's dream is not saying that God gave through the years of plenty and God "taketh away" through the years of scarcity. We live in a fallen world. God was not responsible for the seven years of scarcity; He was responsible for the wisdom that cushioned the blow on the people.

Application more important than Interpretation

We observe that Pharaoh's dreams said nothing about what should be done. Joseph's interpretation also did not say what should be done. Joseph's non-fatalistic interpretation then required a person who was full of the spirit of wisdom to come forth with the application. The spirit of wisdom causes us to see what we should do in every circumstance. The wisdom of God in Joseph's heart looked at Pharaoh's calamity and produced order out of that chaos. Most people would have followed up the interpretation with an application that promotes fear and panic. Since God is not the author of confusion, we know that it would be wrong to say the God-given dream imparted panic.

You see, dreams of themselves do not wreck people. It is people's beliefs, their thinking and their actions that contrive to defeat them. When these three things are wrong, we reap confusion from our dreams or from anything for that matter.

What you do with a dream does not depend on the dream or the content of the dream. It depends on you.

While it is a scary thing to see seven thin cows eat seven fat cows, the spirit of faith interprets so as to stir boldness and confidence. We know that we have arrived at the wrong interpretation of our dream if the interpretation strikes fear in our hearts and robs us of initiative and confidence. First we dream, and then we interpret that dream after which we apply the dream. Only then do we act.

Remember the context of your life

Both the chief butler and the chief baker were in prison because they had broken some royal protocol (see Gen. 40). It is likely that both were worried about what the future would bring. It would appear that the question on their mind could be phrased as, "Would my service to my king be terminated or do I stand a second chance?"

It was against this backdrop that each of these high-ranking officials had a dream.

If you should take your dream seriously at all, there would be a strong correlation between the things happening in your life at a given point in time and the dreams that you have around that time. Too many people try to divorce their dreams from the things happening in their lives around the same time. Our dreams do not just fall out of the sky.

Fellowship with those who interpret dreams well

And he told it to his father, and to his brethren: and his father rebuked
him, and said unto him, What is this dream that thou hast dreamed?
Shall I and thy mother and thy brethren indeed come to bow down
ourselves to thee to the earth?
Genesis 37:10

Notice that Joseph told his dream to his father and his brothers.
It would appear that Jacob's family had the habit of discussing
their dreams. As soon as Joseph told his dream, Jacob assumed
that he knew what it meant. To Jacob, it meant that Jacob and his
wife and children would come to bow down before Joseph who
would rule over them.

And Joseph dreamed a dream, and he told it his brethren: and they hated
him yet the more.
Genesis 37:5

While this is written in a negative way, the underlying lesson is
that their hatred arose from what they understood the dream to
be saying. It would appear that they listened to dreams together
and discerned its meaning together. It would appear that their
fellowship with one another caused them to interpret dreams
and arrive at similar conclusions. This was how they sharpened
this ability.

And there was there with us a young man, an Hebrew, servant to the
captain of the guard; and we told him, and he interpreted to us our
dreams; to each man according to his dream he did interpret. And it
came to pass, as he interpreted to us, so it was; me he restored unto mine
office, and him he hanged. Then Pharaoh sent and called Joseph, and
they brought him hastily out of the dungeon: and he shaved himself, and

changed his raiment, and came in unto Pharaoh.
Genesis 41:12-14

Joseph developed this ability to interpret dreams to such a degree that he could interpret the dreams of others. He did this so accurately that when Pharaoh had his dream and none of the other established guys could interpret it, Joseph was the one that was called upon. He had developed it beyond what was initiated in his father's house.

As for these four children, God gave them knowledge and skill in all
learning and wisdom: and Daniel had understanding in all visions and
dreams.
Daniel 1:17

We also notice that Daniel and his friends had the gift for interpreting visions and dreams. This group of men fellowshipped together, rubbed off on one another and sharpened this ability to understand and interpret dreams.

It was not a case of one man laying hands upon the other in order that they might receive the ability to interpret dreams. It is God that gives that ability. We are to trust God for the operation of the spirit of wisdom and revelation as we trust the unction from the Holy One to teach us all things. This way we become more skill in interpreting our own dreams.

Preparing to Sleep

Dream scientists tell us that during what they call the alpha sleep stage, our eyes and our brains respond as though they were watching action scenes in a movie. The brain is highly active during the dream stage because it is analysing the dream input as though we were experiencing it in real life. Some people think this allows the mind to recalibrate and rest so we can remain sane, maintain psychological balance and focus excellently when awake. Sleep scientists have found that nervous breakdown sets in if a person is prevented from entering the Rapid eye Movement phase three days in a row. Thus dreaming is not as trivial as it might seem at first glance.

Given all that happens when we sleep we ought to approach sleep in a spiritually intelligent way.

Too many Christians are body conscious only; therefore, they assume that their day is over when they drift off into sleep.

We should prepare to sleep just as much as we prepare for

everything else in life. Your body might have stopped moving around while asleep but the day is far from over. Solomon's encounter with God was in a dream. His spirit was having spiritual experiences while his body was asleep. We should really think of sleeping as entering into another phase of our day.

I will both lay me down in peace, and sleep: for thou, LORD, only makest me dwell in safety.
Psalm 4:8

Letting the peace of God put you to sleep is a more scriptural expression of faith than entertaining anxiety in unbelief while trying to pray. Praying with anxiety pressures away the safety that God has already supplied through His grace. He has given to us the privilege of receiving safety as His gift to us. We rest calmly in His provision.

Fill your thoughts with God's Word before you go to sleep. If you do not know what to think, rather than paralyzing yourself with fear and anxiety, think about yourself lying down in peace. As you make God's Word your thought, the peace of God is released from your spirit to your soul and body.

There is a wonderful piece of scripture in Proverbs about sleep.

When thou liest down, thou shalt not be afraid: yea, thou shalt lie down, and thy sleep shall be sweet.
Proverbs 3:24

There is a relationship between sweet sleep and the fear that we entertain in our lives. What many people end up dreaming are their fears and anxieties replayed at night and projected upon their soul. God's Word has the ability to completely rinse off fear from our heart.

If we are not restful enough to enter into deep sleep, we might limit ourselves from receiving peace flowing out of our spirits to protect our heart and minds.

When you are full of God's Word, you don't need to put up with a night of troublesome dreams. The Word of God spoken out of your mouth creates a supernaturally charged atmosphere. In such an atmosphere the Spirit is given free flow and the manifest presence of God is stronger. This causes the power of God to linger upon you and your dreams have a different element to them. You should practice those things that fill your atmosphere with God's manifest presence before you drift off into sleep. In that type of atmosphere, you calmly close your eyes, enter into the dream arena and call a bluff on anything the enemy could throw your way. God's Word makes you equally dangerous awake or asleep because the DNA of victory still resides within.

The bible shows the tremendous power of the thoughts that we think just before we drift off into sleep.

But while he thought on these things, behold, the angel of the LORD appeared unto him in a dream, saying, Joseph, thou son of David, fear not to take unto thee Mary thy wife: for that which is conceived in her is of the Holy Ghost.
Matthew 1:20

Joseph was so engrossed in how to execute his decision to put away Mary that while thinking about it, he fell asleep. He was seeking a strategy for ending their relationship (see Mt. 1:20). Then the angel appeared to him in a dream. His dream was linked to the thoughts that had troubled his mind the night before he had drifted into sleep. This validates the point that we cannot be tempted by anything that we do not allow to persist in our thought life. This is also true of our dreams. If Joseph had not filled his mind with those thoughts he would likely have dreamt a different set of dreams that night. In a way, we affect our own dreams.

As for thee, O king, thy thoughts came into thy mind upon thy bed, what should come to pass hereafter: and he that revealeth secrets maketh known to thee what shall come to pass.
Daniel 2:29

This shows that the thoughts that we nurture as we prepare to sleep are important. Nebuchadnezzar's thoughts before he went to sleep were centered on the future and what lay on the horizon of time. These filtered through his heart into his dreams. He ended up being given the answer to his thoughts in the form of a dream.

It is a well-known fact that providing we absorb plenty of data in our waking moments; while we are asleep another mind goes to work that makes sense of what our conscious mind has struggled with. This does not happen often enough in people who are not given to thinking things through. It is through this process that the noted scientist, August Kekule, was shown the structure of benzene in a dream. This was also how Mendeleev discovered, in a dream, the periodic table, which allows scientists logically organize chemical elements. When we are asleep, this other intelligence in man continues to work on issues that have stumped our conscious mind.

Sweet sleep by saying

And the Lord said, If ye had faith as a grain of mustard seed, ye might say unto this sycamine tree, Be thou plucked up by the root, and be thou planted in the sea; and it should obey you.
Luke 17:6

The Lord Jesus said that the sycamore tree would obey you. He did not say that it would obey God; therefore don't tell God to speak to the sycamore tree on your behalf. If it were up to God He would have uprooted it with the word of His mouth long ago.

Clearly Jesus wasn't talking about horticulture, was He? Jesus was talking about how we uproot bitterness and fear from our hearts, by the words of our mouth. We use our mouths to pluck the root of bitterness and fear.

Spiritual power is released primarily through words. Whenever we speak, we are giving expression to spiritual things. These things that we say out of our mouths take root within our hearts and ultimately programs our hearts to agree with what we have spoken. This is true even if the thing released through words is wrong.

Utterances are the doorway into the fullness of God. You'll notice that the sequence starts with utterance in the form of tongues and interpretation in particular, which then leads to visions and dreams.

This principle will work for erasing the power of bitterness and fear so you can receive sweet sleep as an operation of God's grace.

God has already given us sweet sleep; bitterness and fear stops us from receiving it.

Learn to use the words of your mouth to prepare your heart just before you sleep. Nothing prepares your heart like the words of your mouth. Quit saying, "My dreams are fuzzy, unclear and useless." If you speak that way, you will soon believe it and then you'll have what you say. Your heart will work so as to help you reap what you have spoken with your mouth and believed.. A fuzzy heart encourages fuzzy dreams.

Why not say out loud to yourself,

My eye is single and my mind is pure.
When I lie down to sleep, my sleep is sweet
God fills the eyes of my heart with beautiful and powerful expressions of
His might when I lay down in sleep.
The unction within brings me understanding, clarity and light tonight.
My heart awakens me so I can recall the leadings of God with ease.

OTHER BOOKS BY AUTHOR

All books available on Amazon
Contact Author
sekou@sekou.me